ZAGREB
Photo Journal

Robert Ornig

Copyright © 2019 by Robert Orniq

All rights reserved. This book or any portion thereof
may not be reproduced or used in any manner whatsoever
without the express written permission of the publisher
except for the use of brief quotations in a book review.
Printed in the United States of America

ZAGREB

PHOTO JOURNAL
BY ROBERT ORNIG

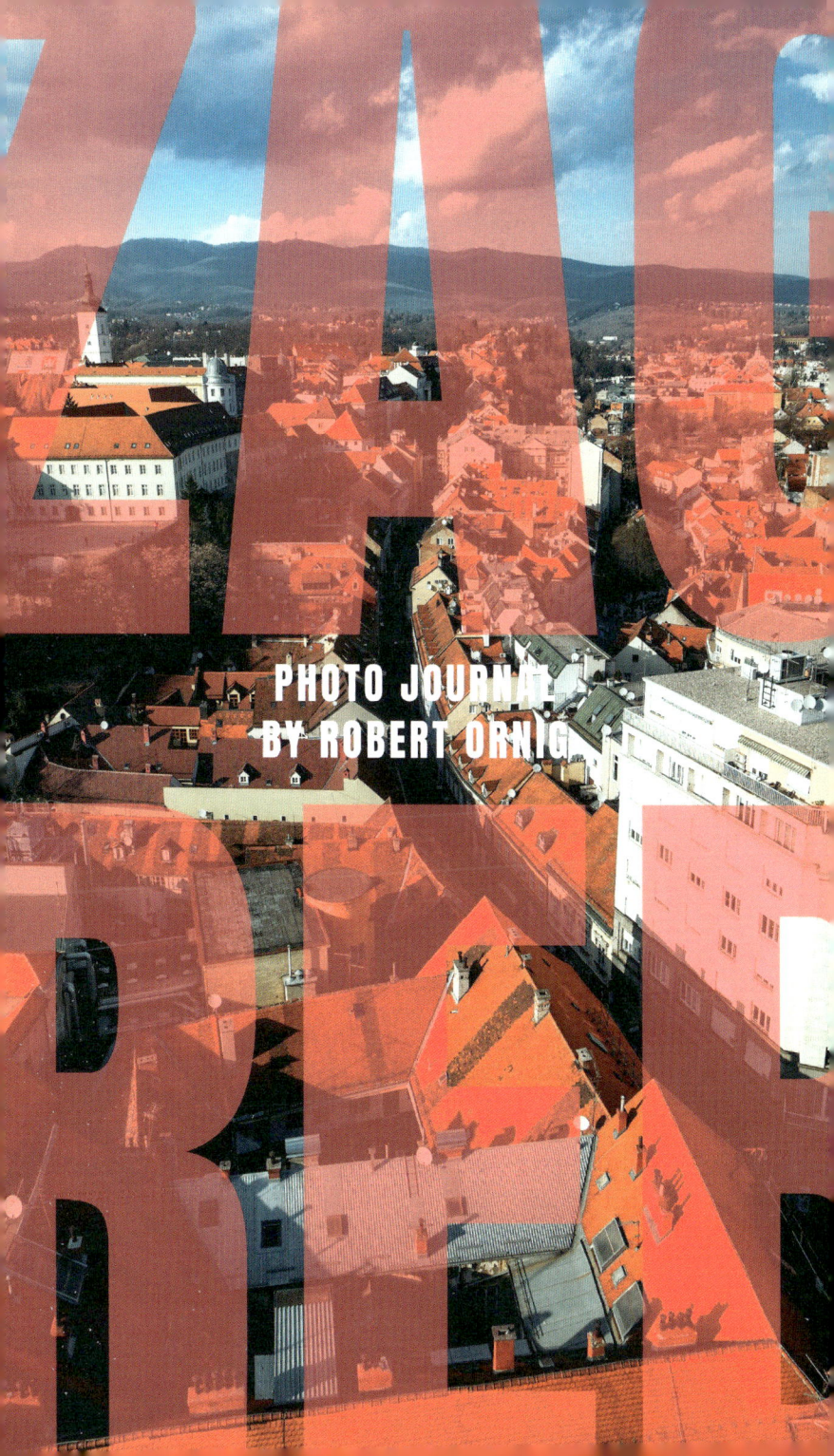

To my mother Robyn for her support and guidance, this book is affectionately dedicated.

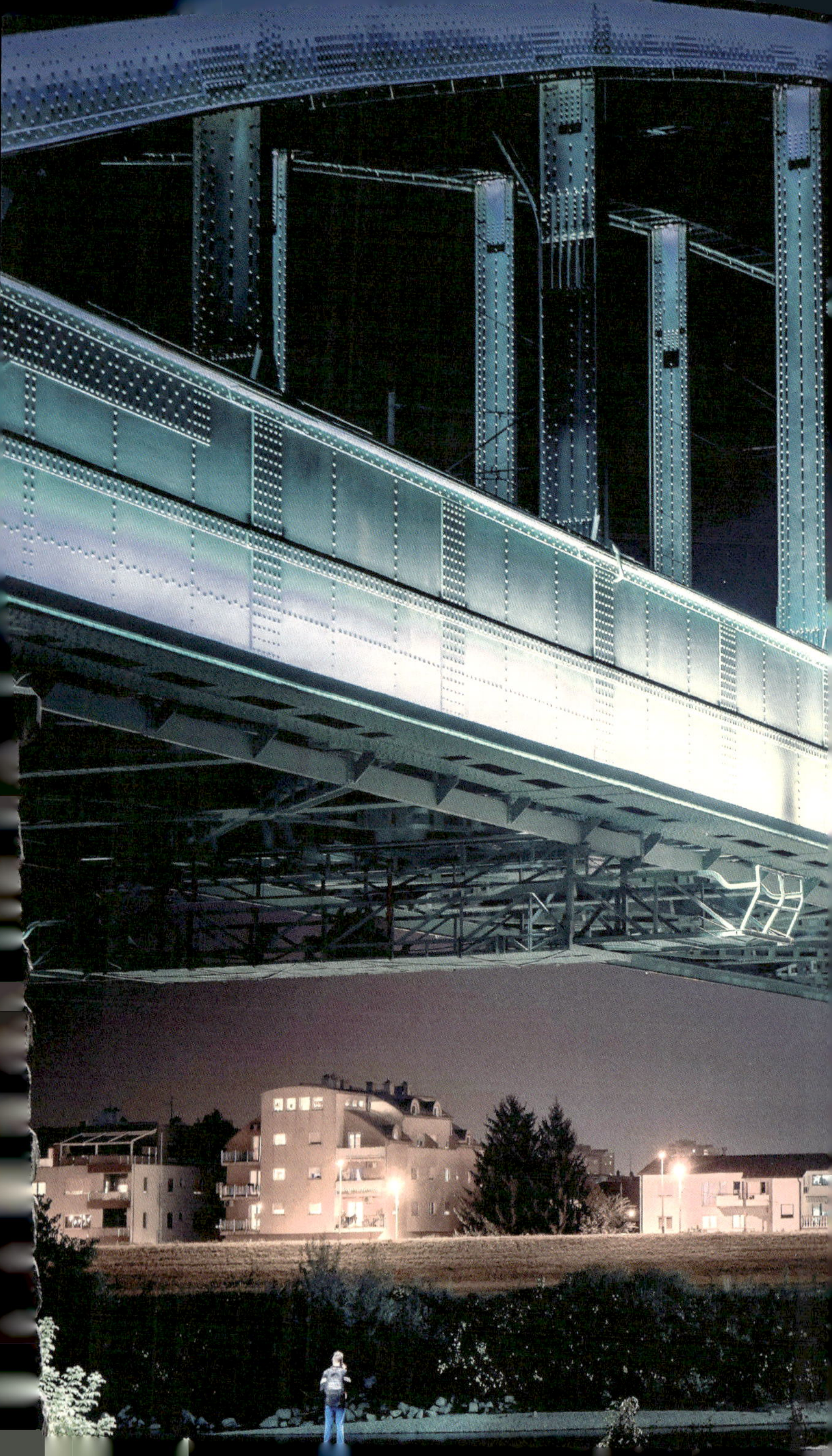

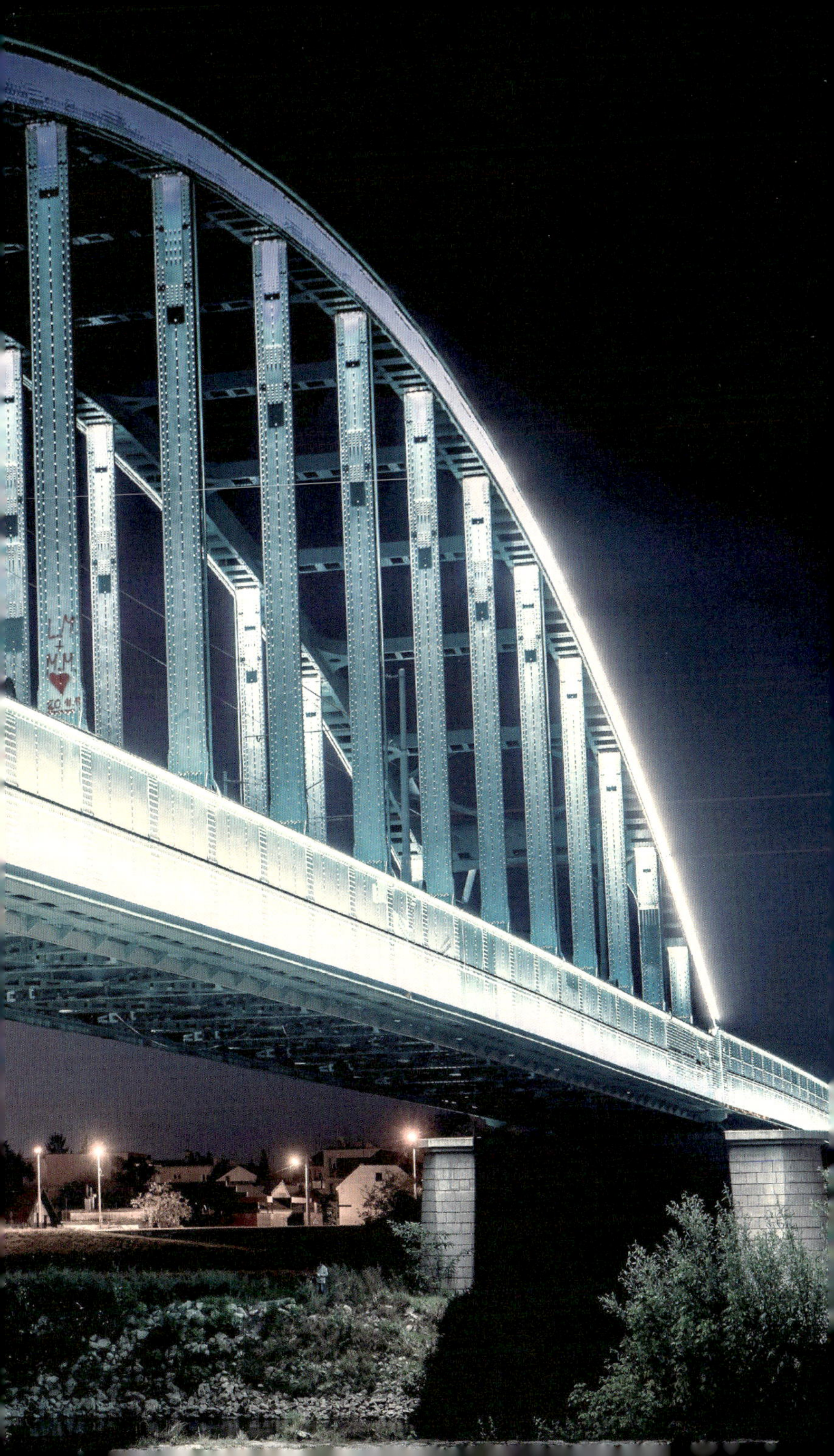

Standing on the cusp of central and western Europe, straddling the historical and the modern, Zagreb is full of stories and monuments that mark the passage of time. Divided into lower and upper towns, Old Zagreb is quite compact and almost all the sights are within walking distance. The Lower Town (Donji Grad) is a grid of beautiful Baroque buildings housing museums and galleries, characterized by the influence of the Austro-Hungarian empire interspersed with lovely green parks, while the hilly Upper Town, accessed by a quaint and pretty funicular, is marked by a plethora of churches, cobblestoned streets and the distinctive feel of a bygone era with gas street lamps and the heaviness of history.

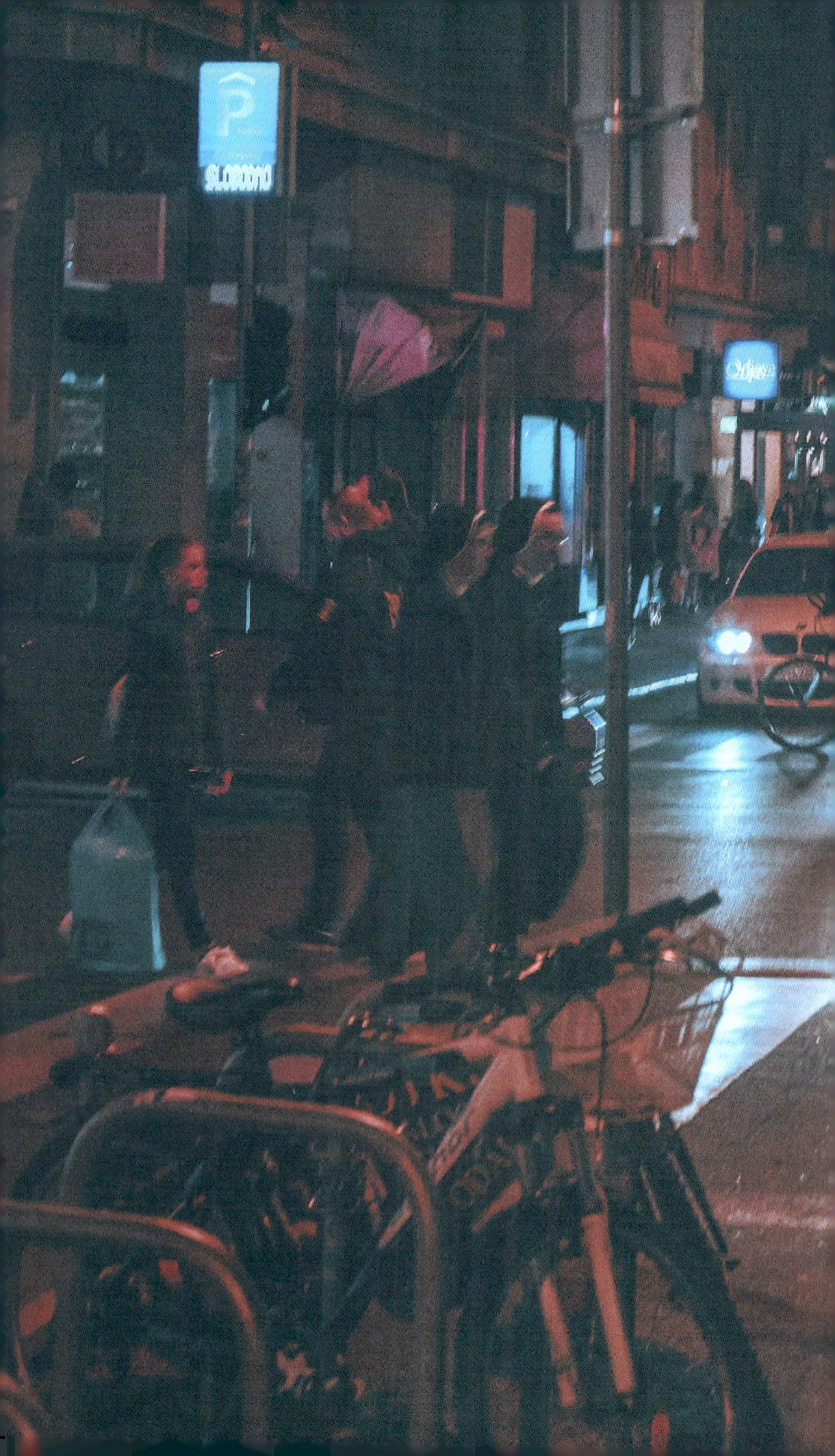

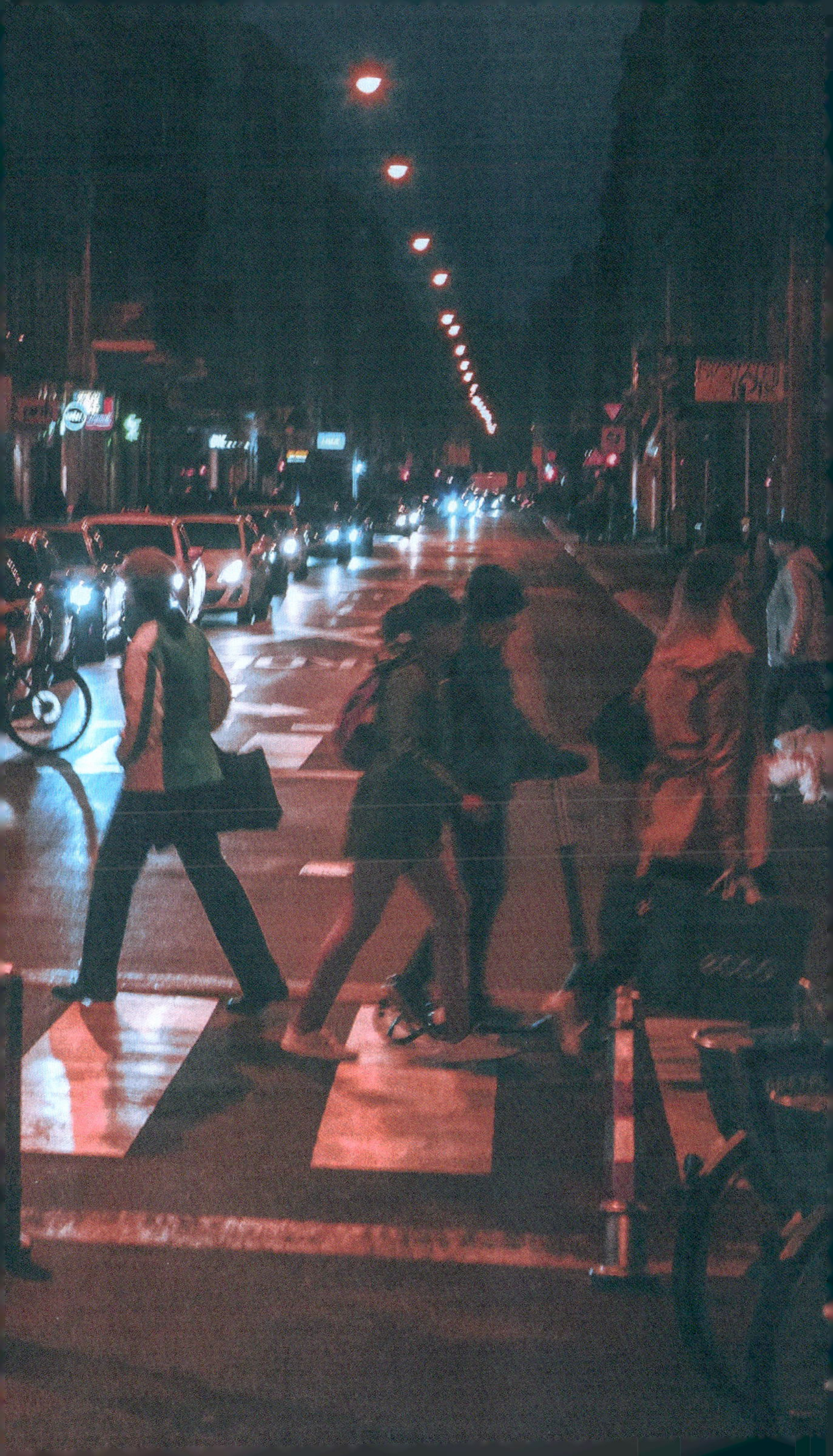

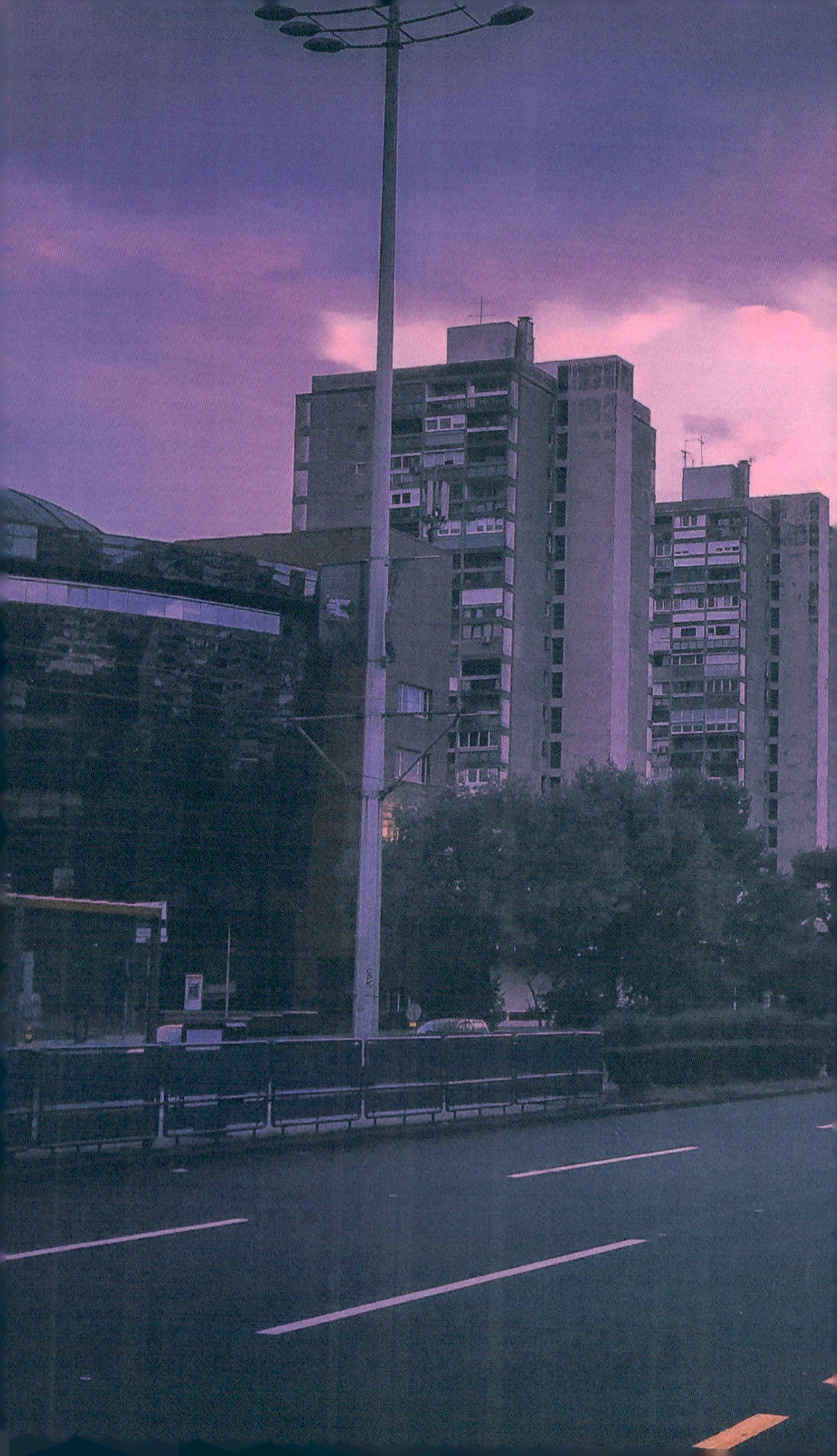

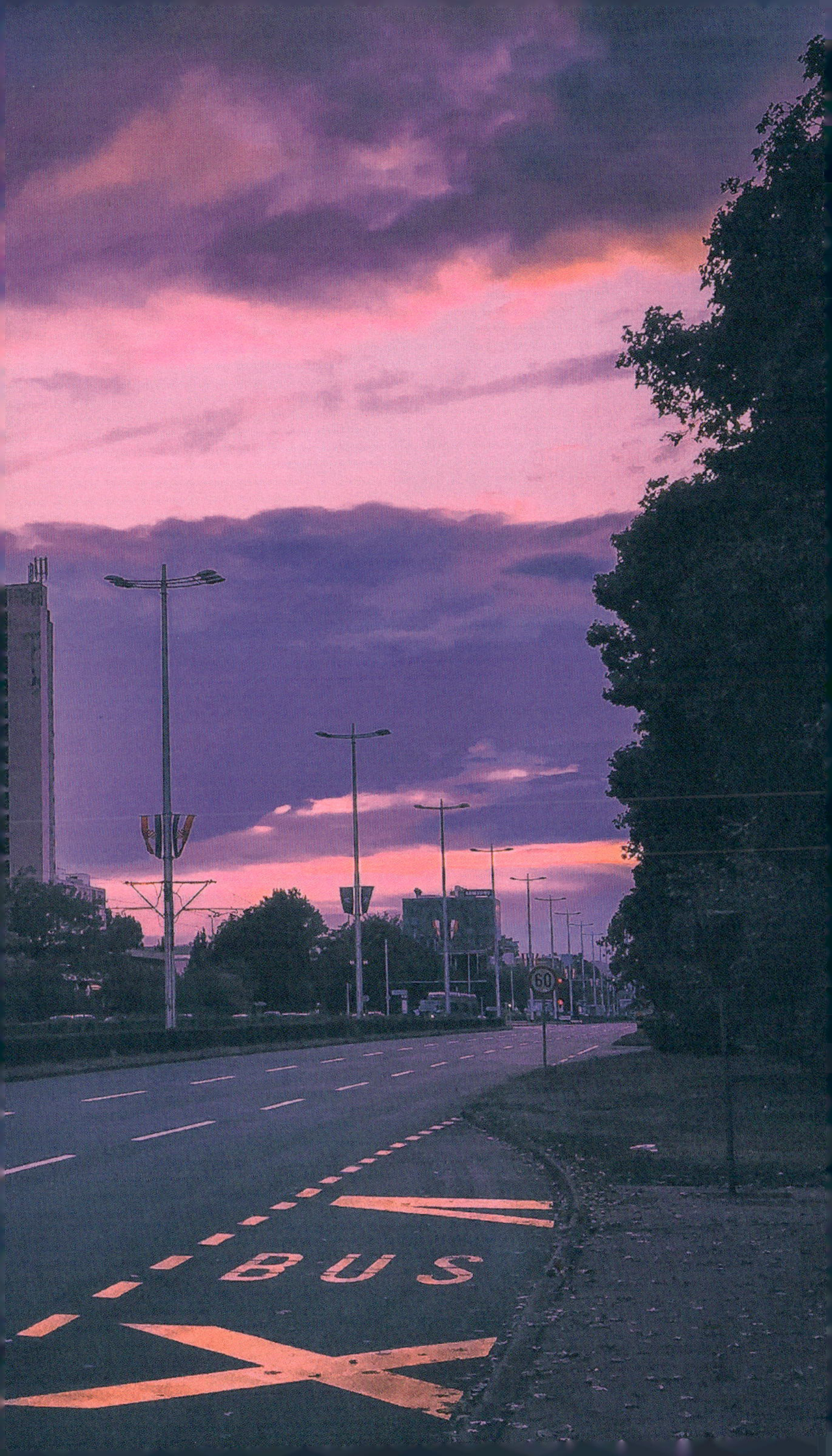
60
BUS

"A nomad I will remain for life, in love with distant and uncharted places."
Isabelle Eberhardt

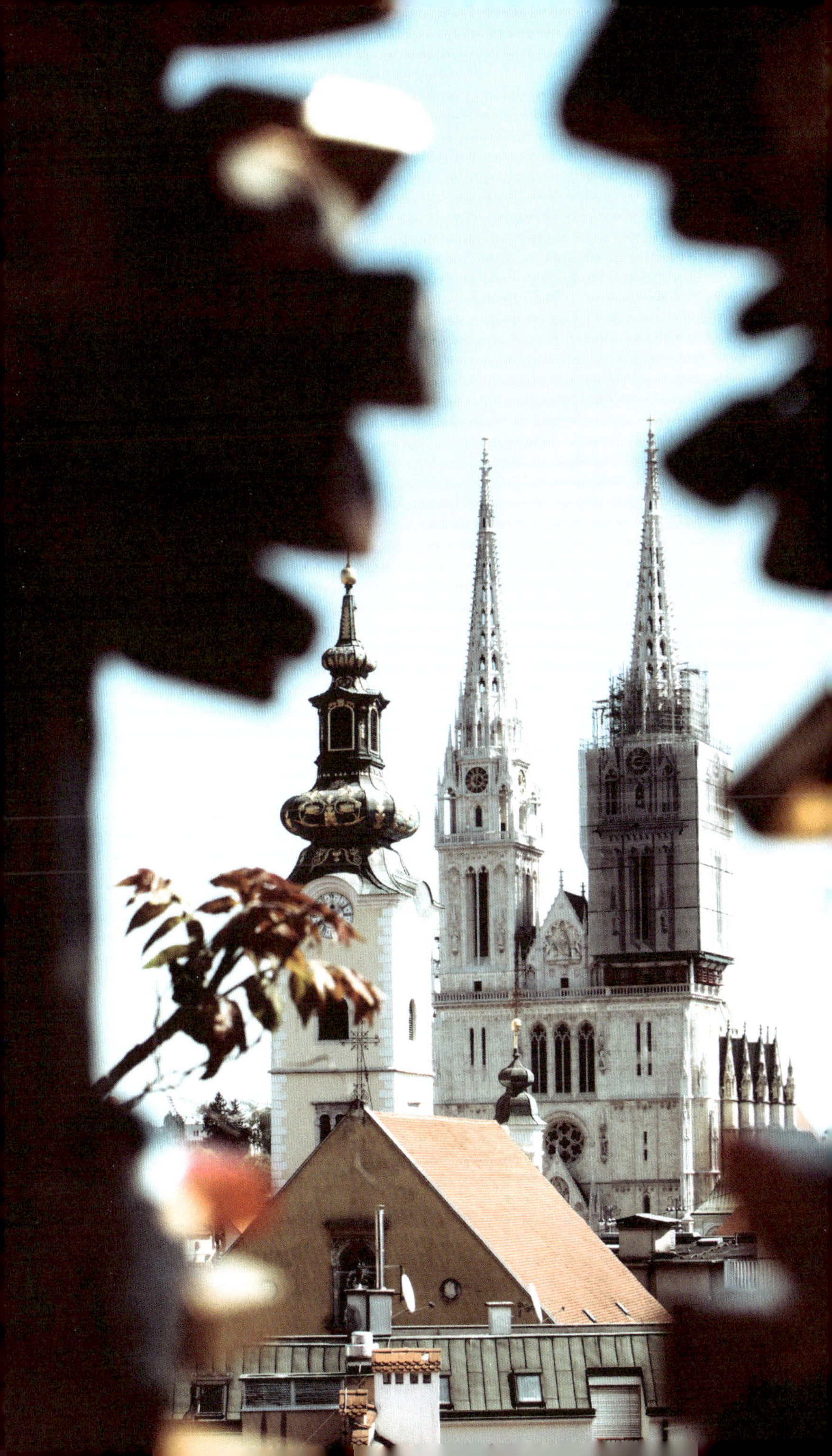

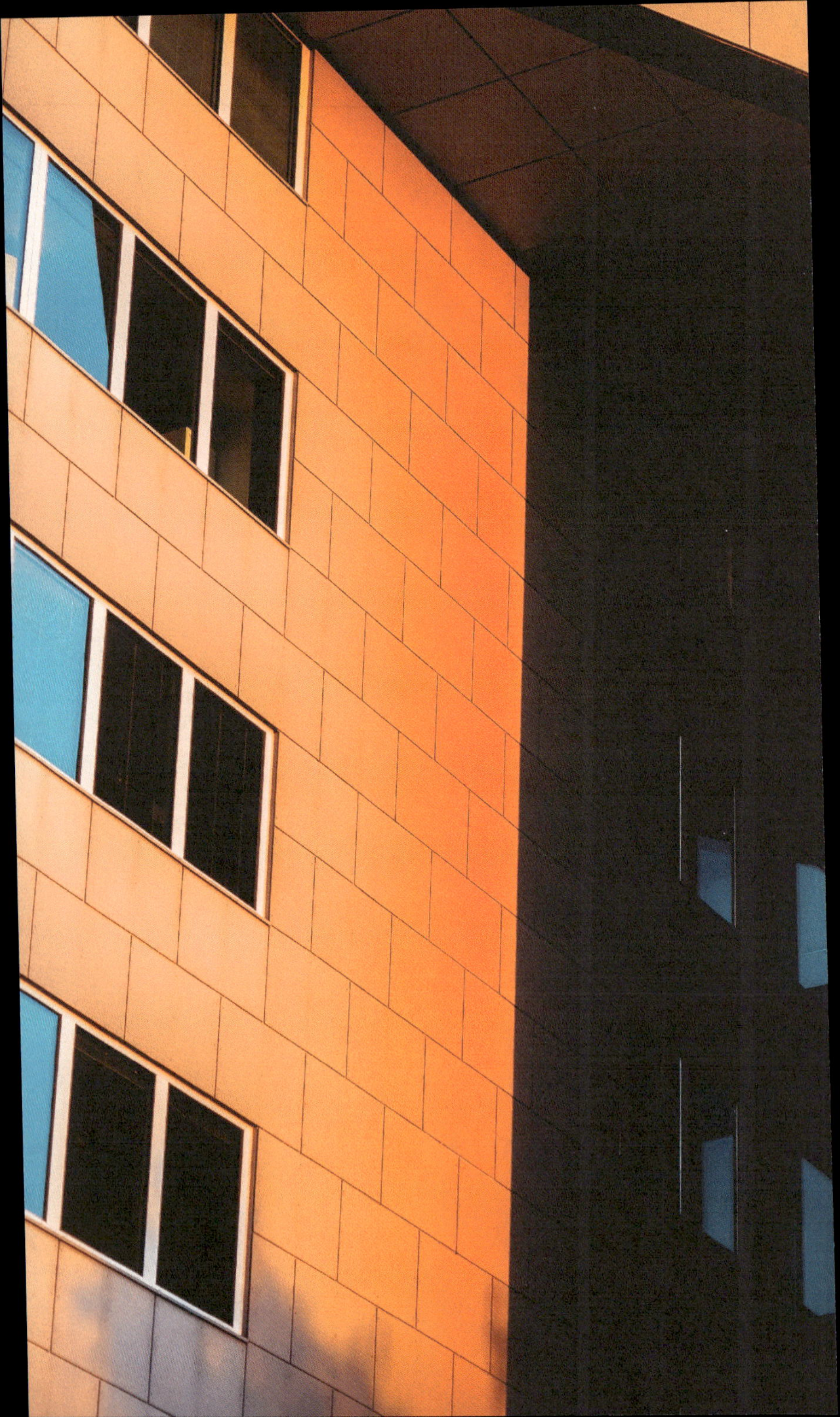

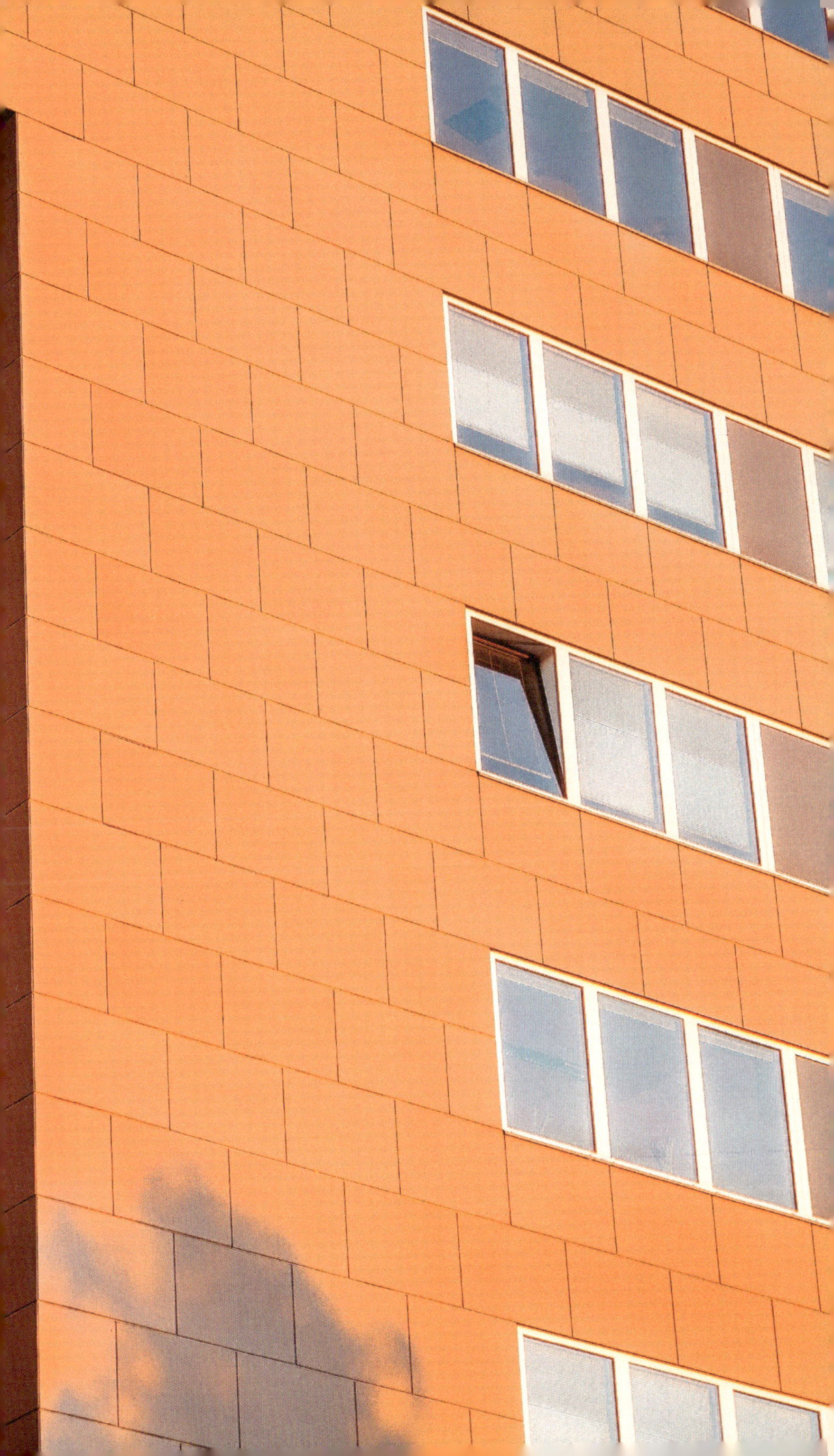

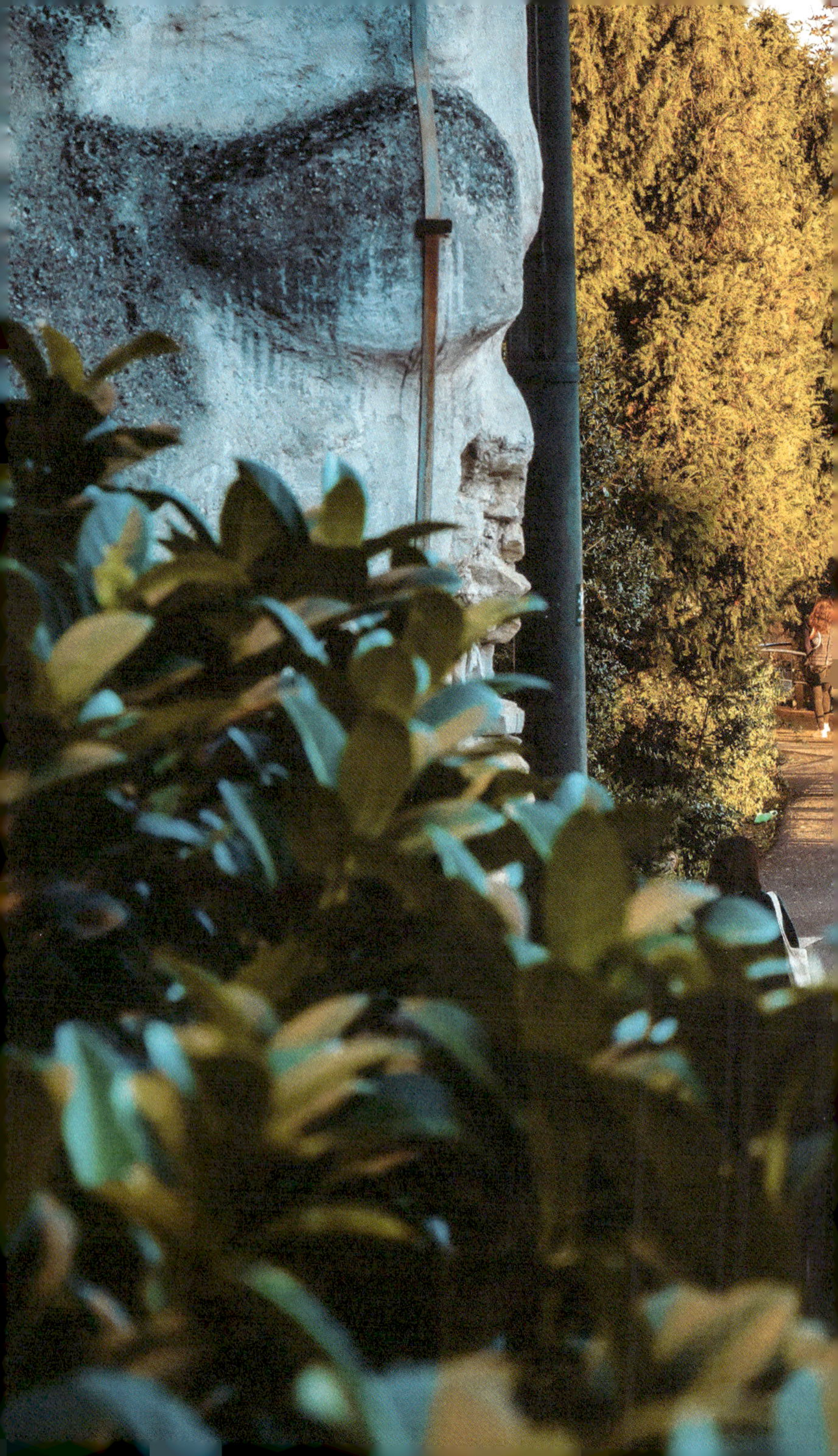

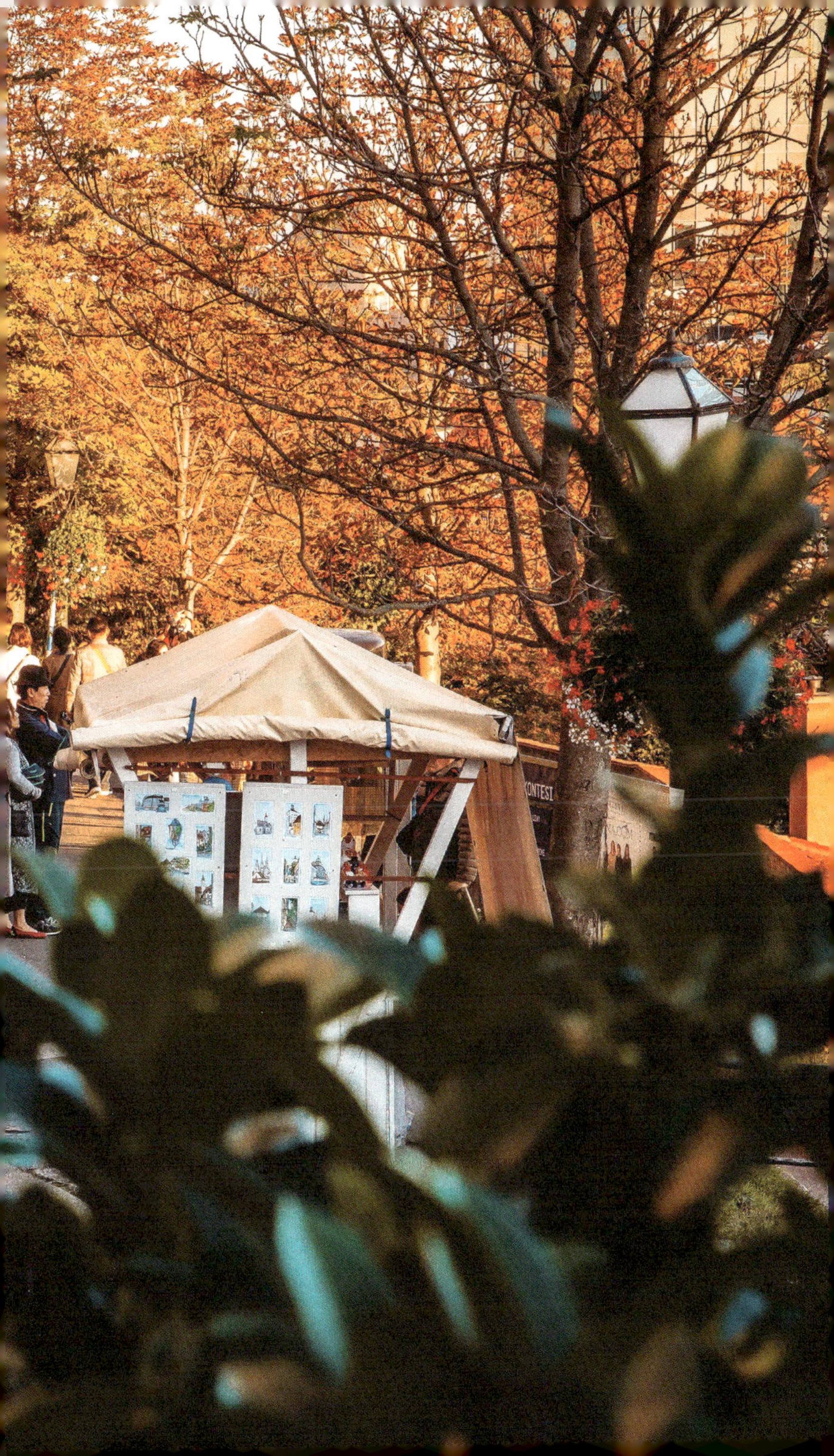

"Photography is the story I fail to put into words."
Destin Sparks

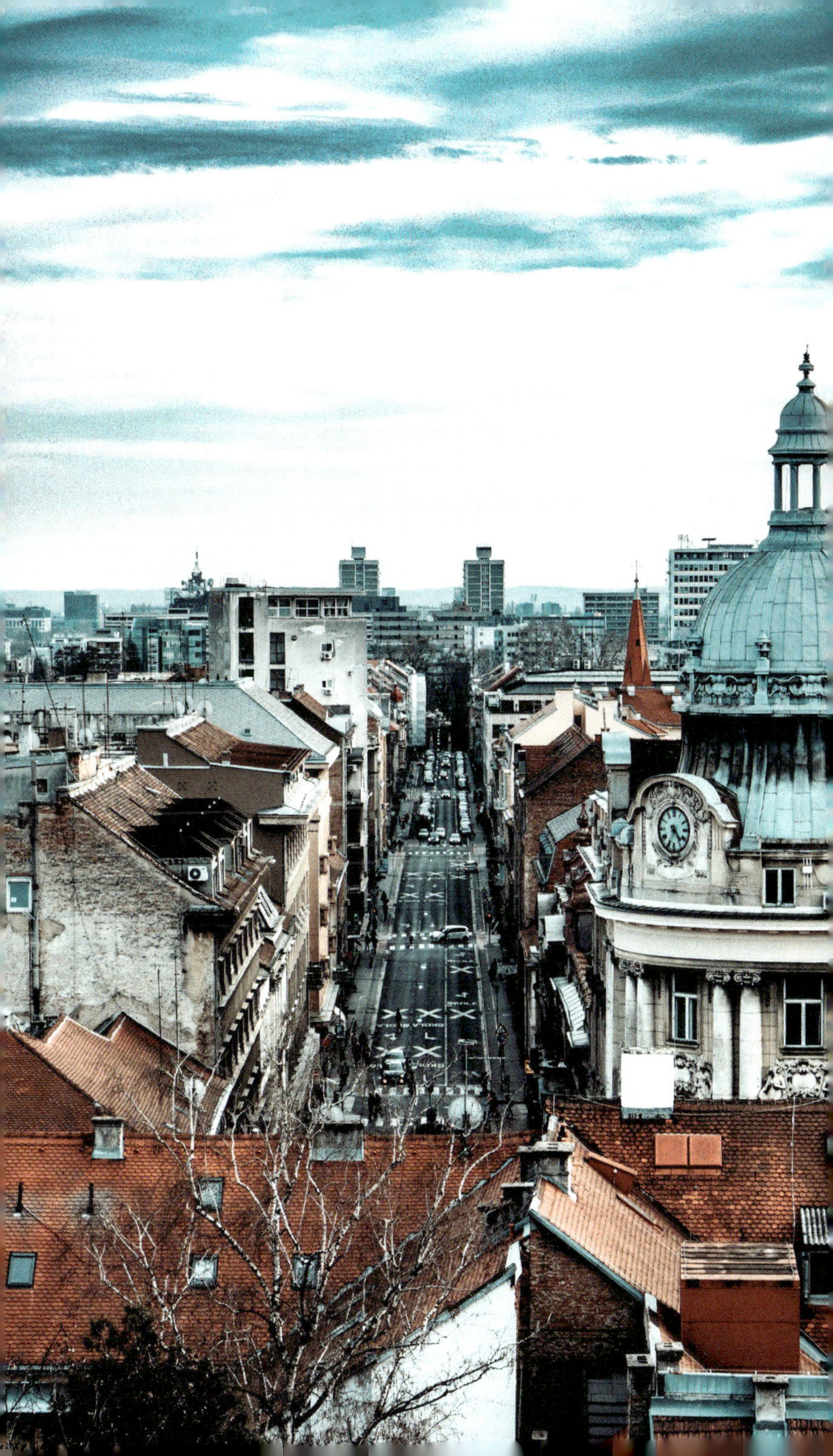

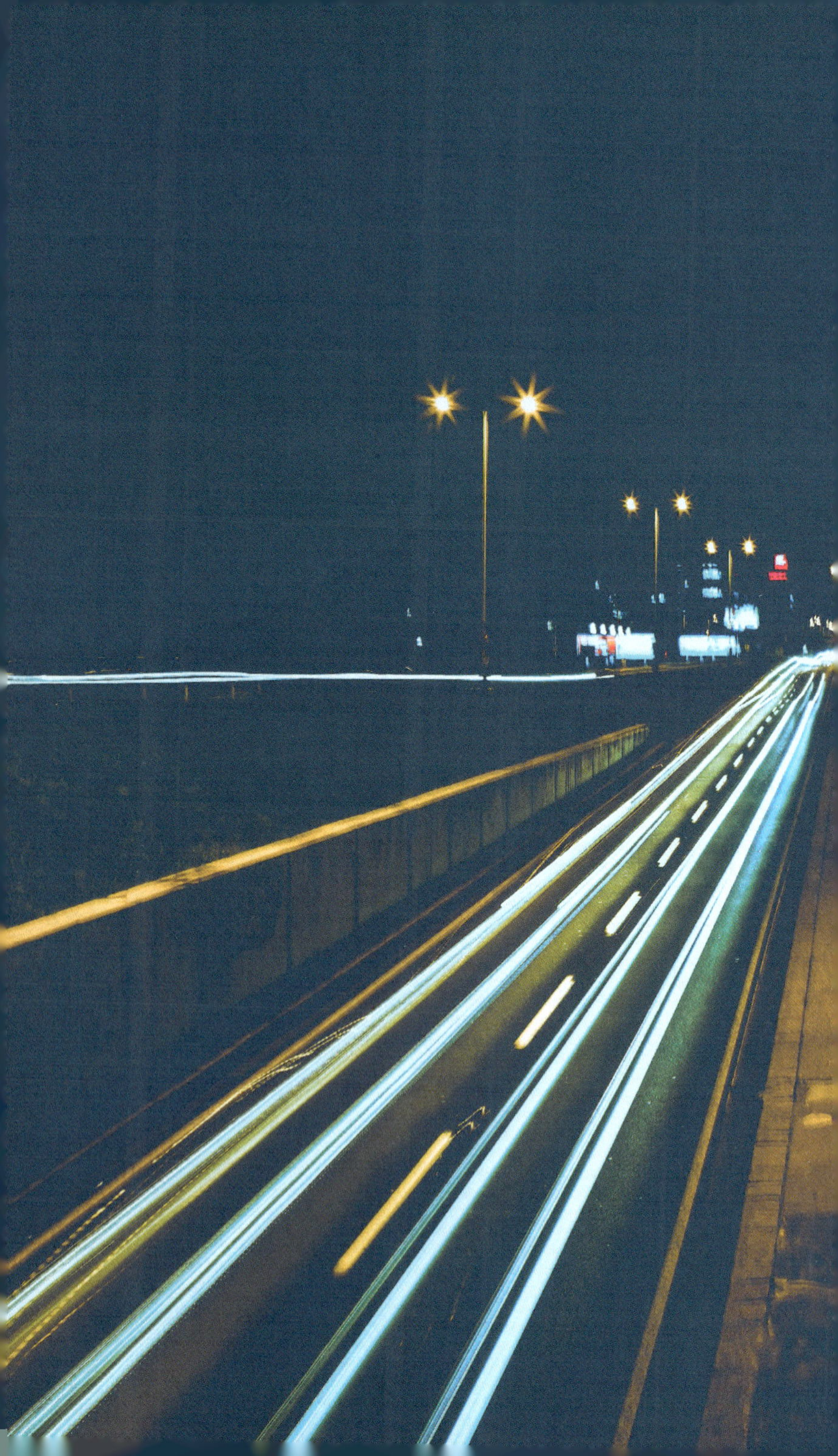

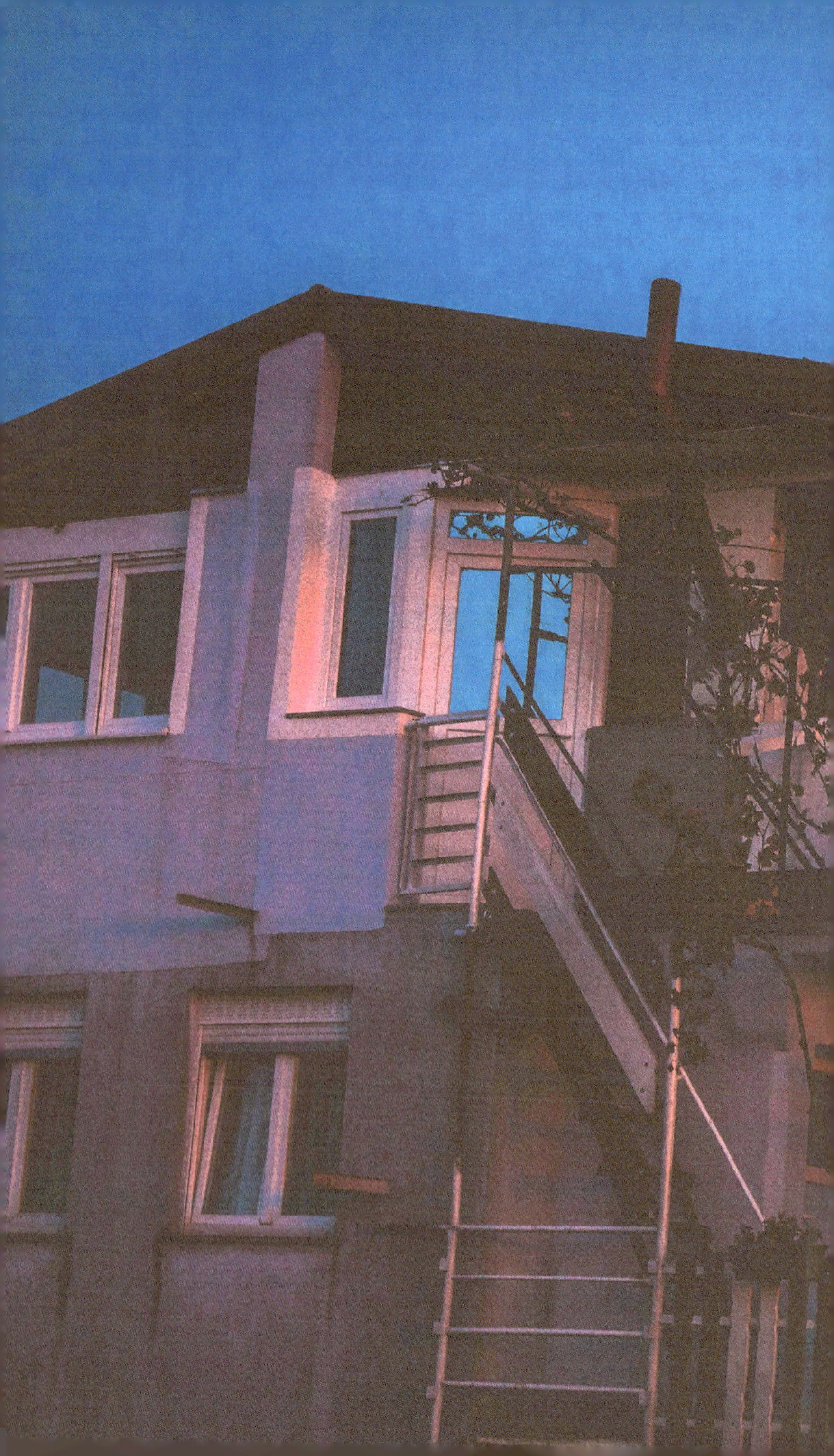

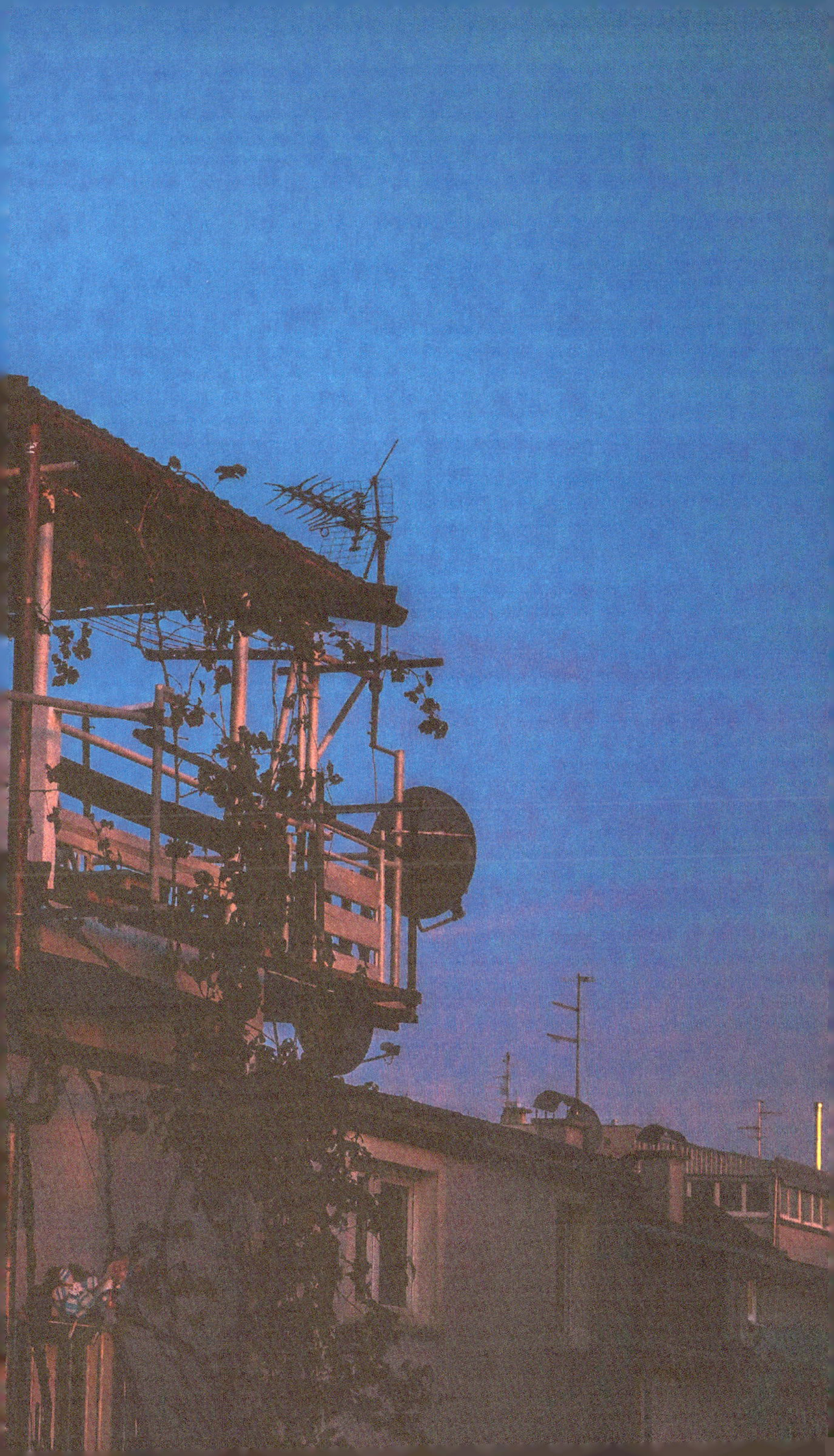

"Taking an image, freezing a moment, reveals how rich reality truly is."
Anonymous

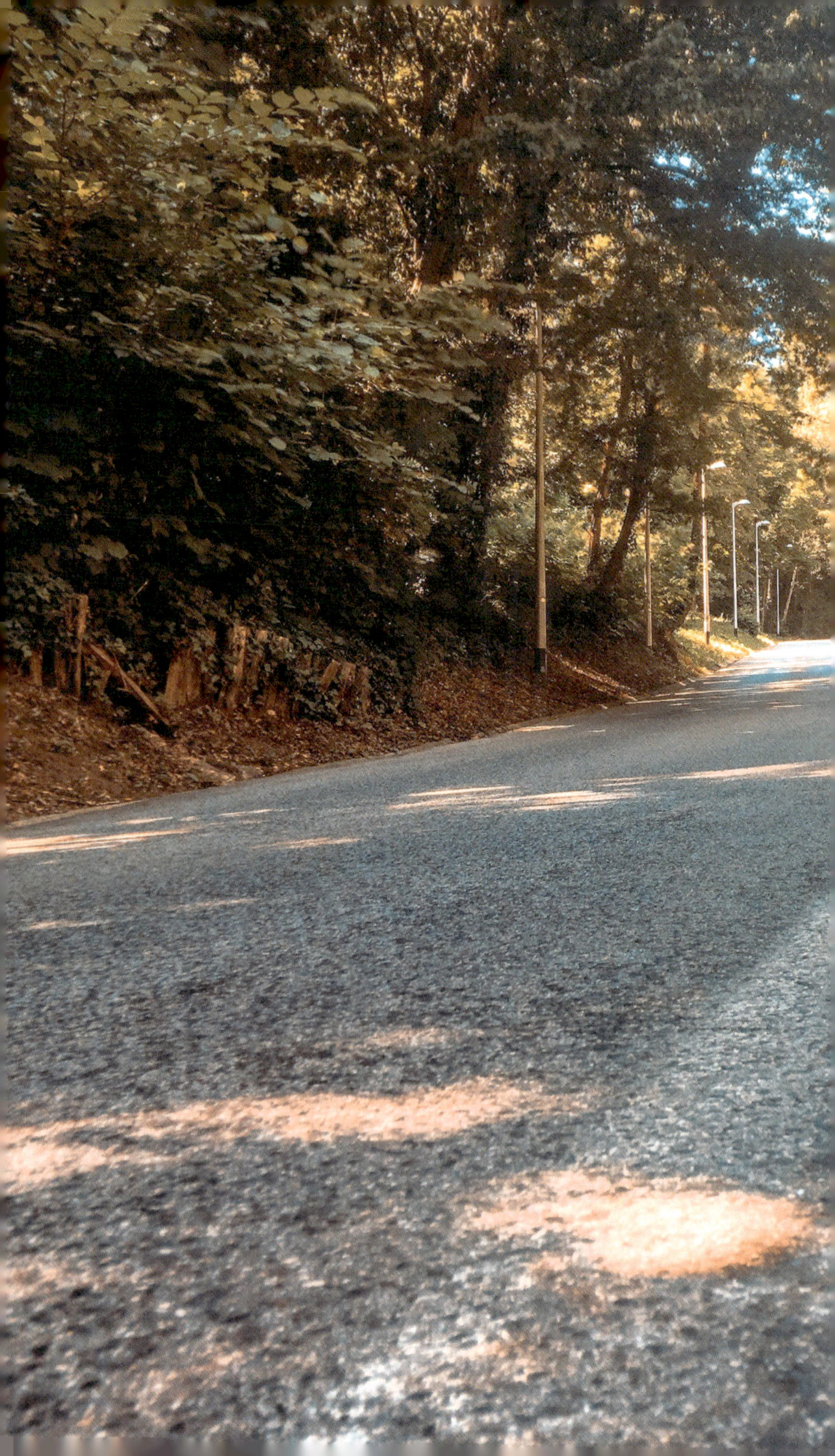

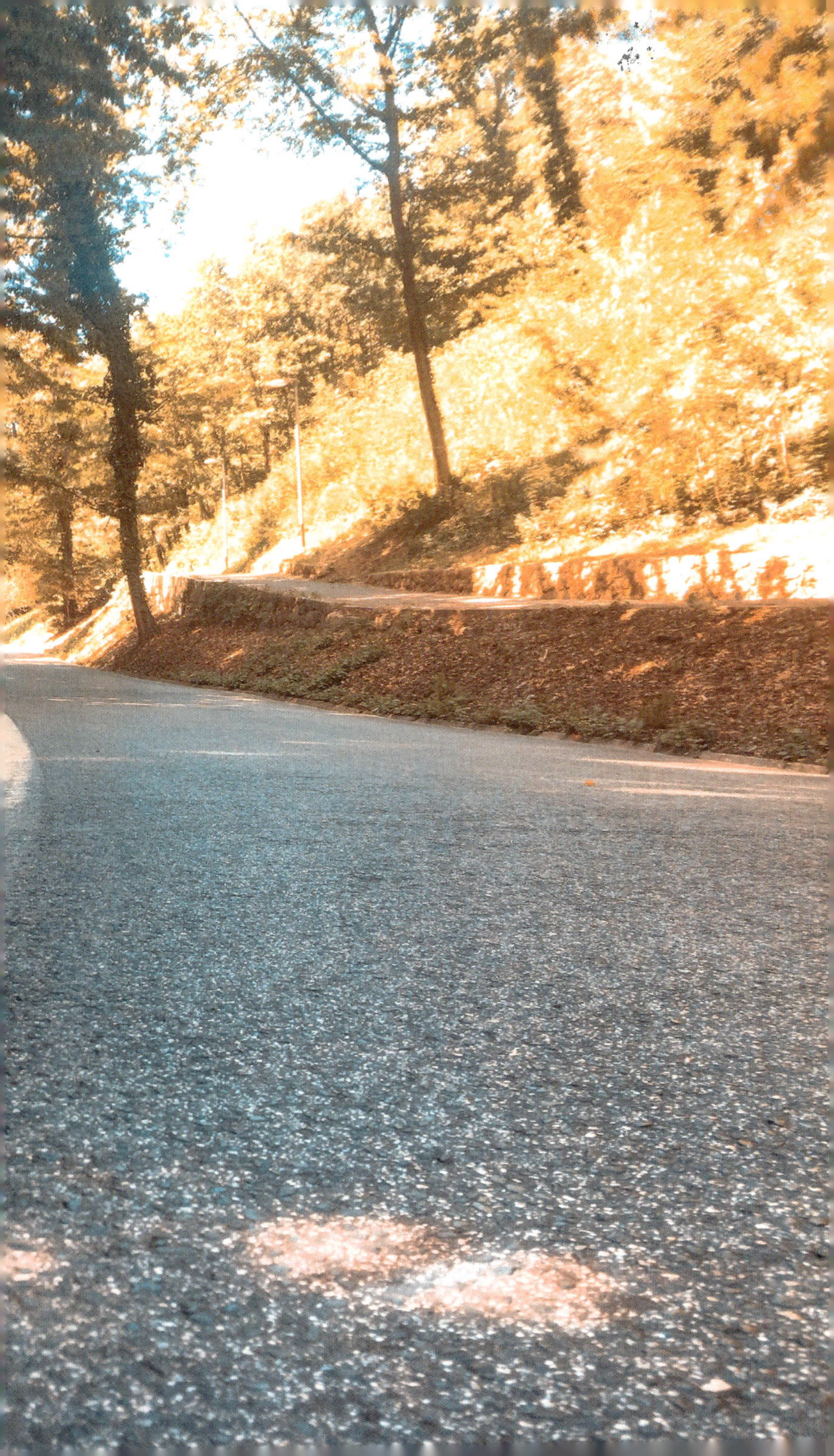

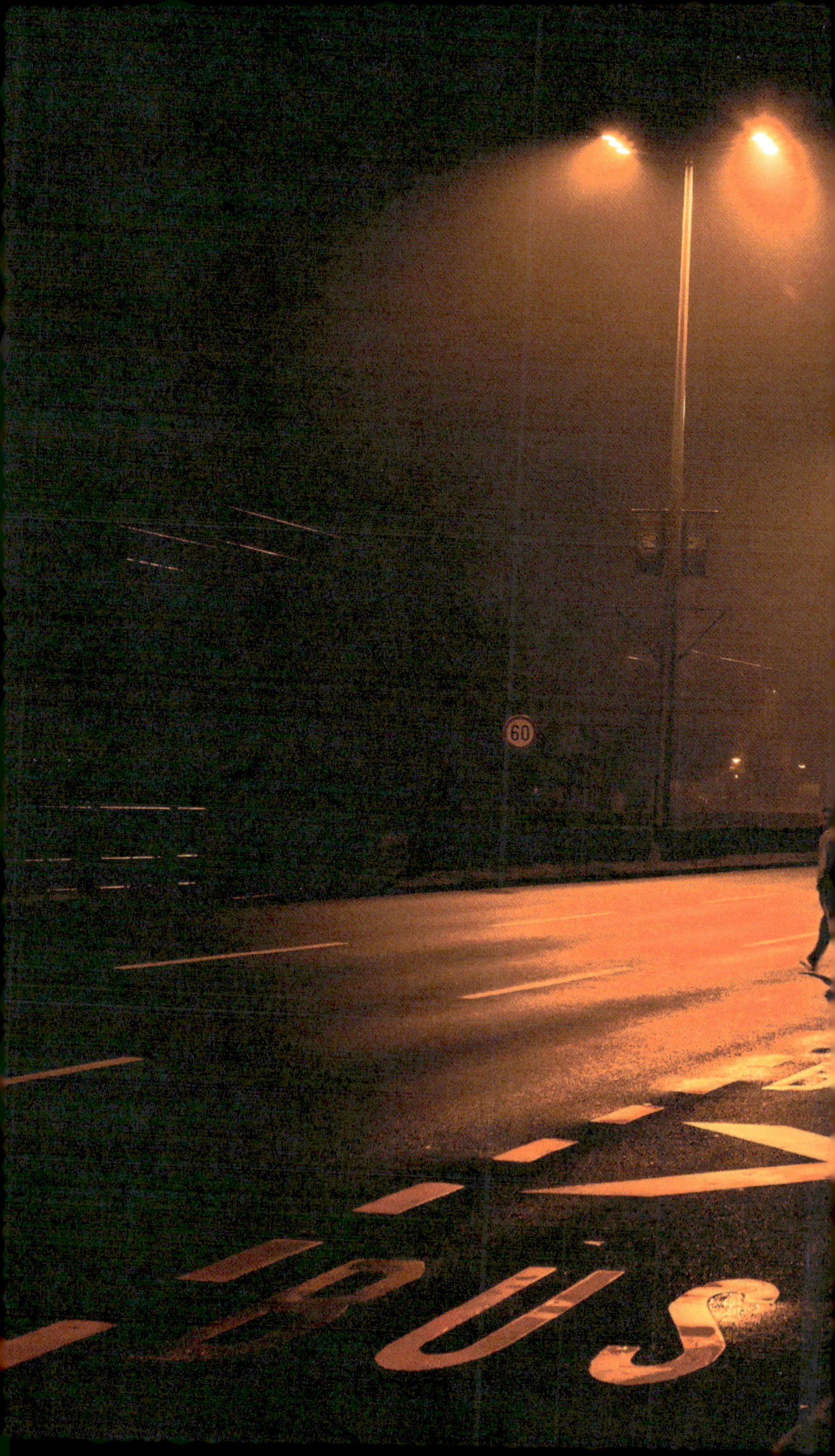
60
BUS

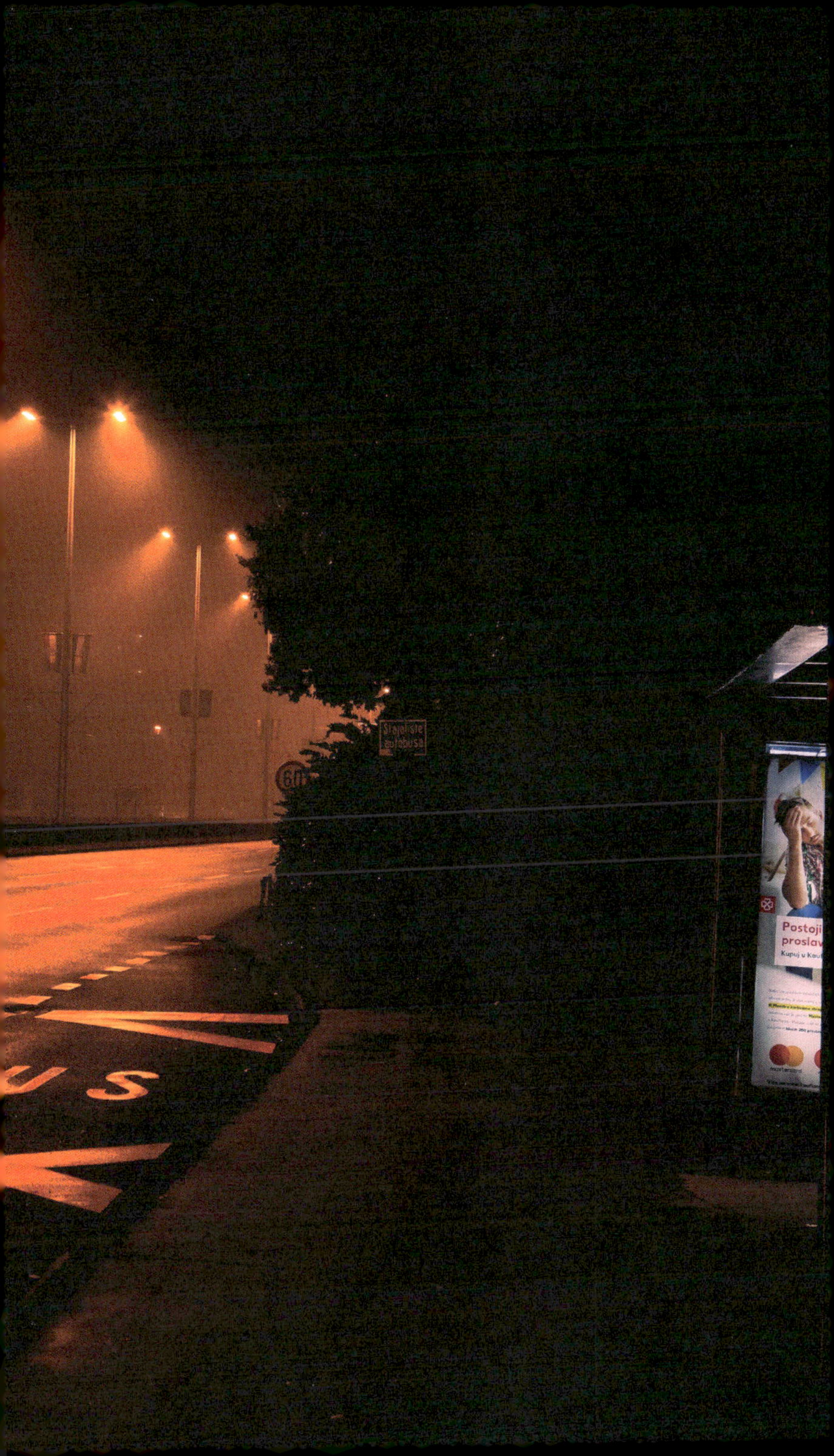
60
US
Postoji

"I don't trust words. I trust pictures."
Gilles Peress

RESTAURANT
BAR & RESTAURANT
Store
comma,
dm
KONZUM
BAR & BISTROT

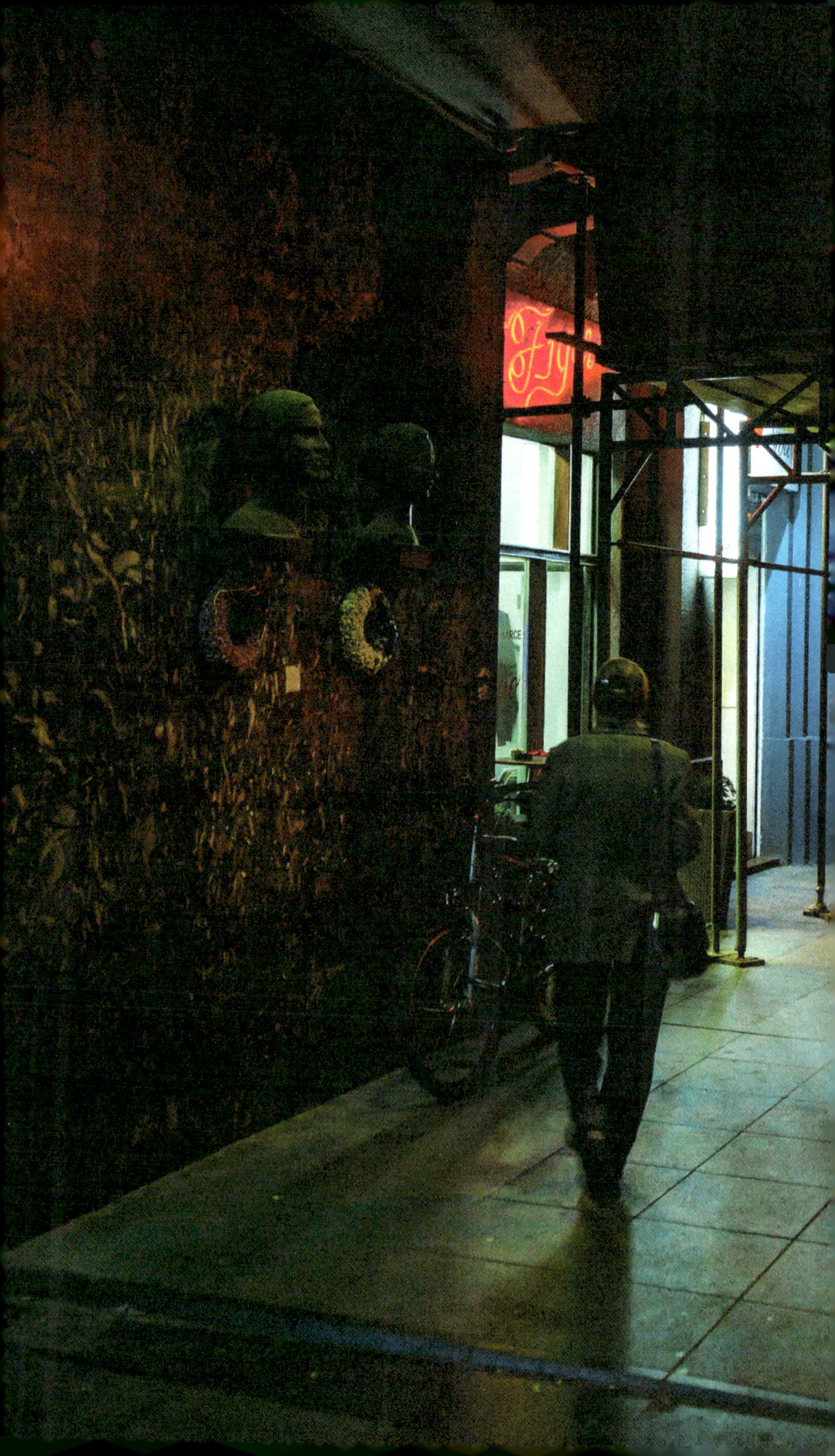

EUROPA
EUROPA
EUROPA
EUROPA
EUROPA

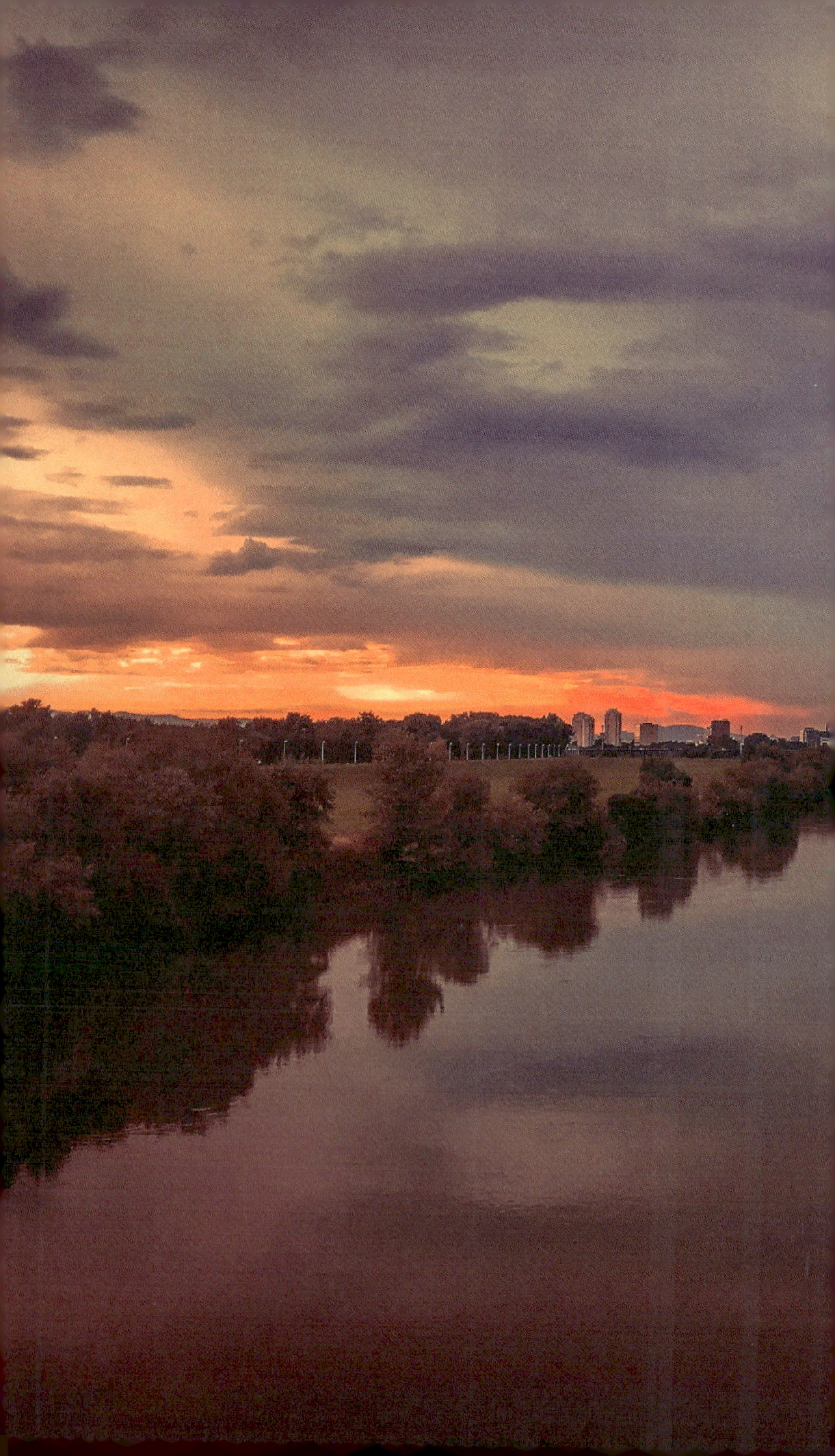

"There are two types of nomads. Those who belong everywhere and those who belong nowhere."
Anonymous

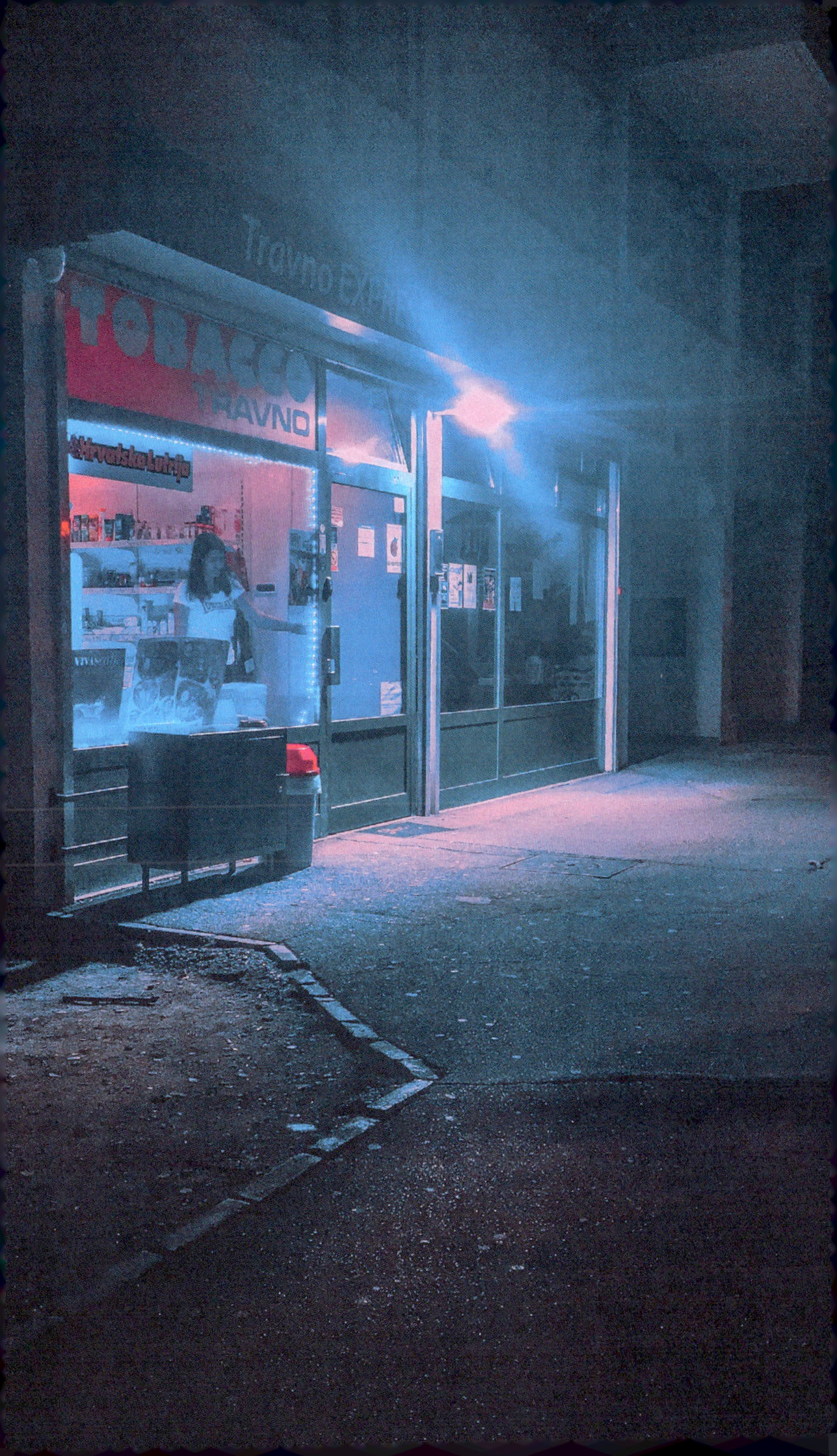
TOBACCO
TRAVNO

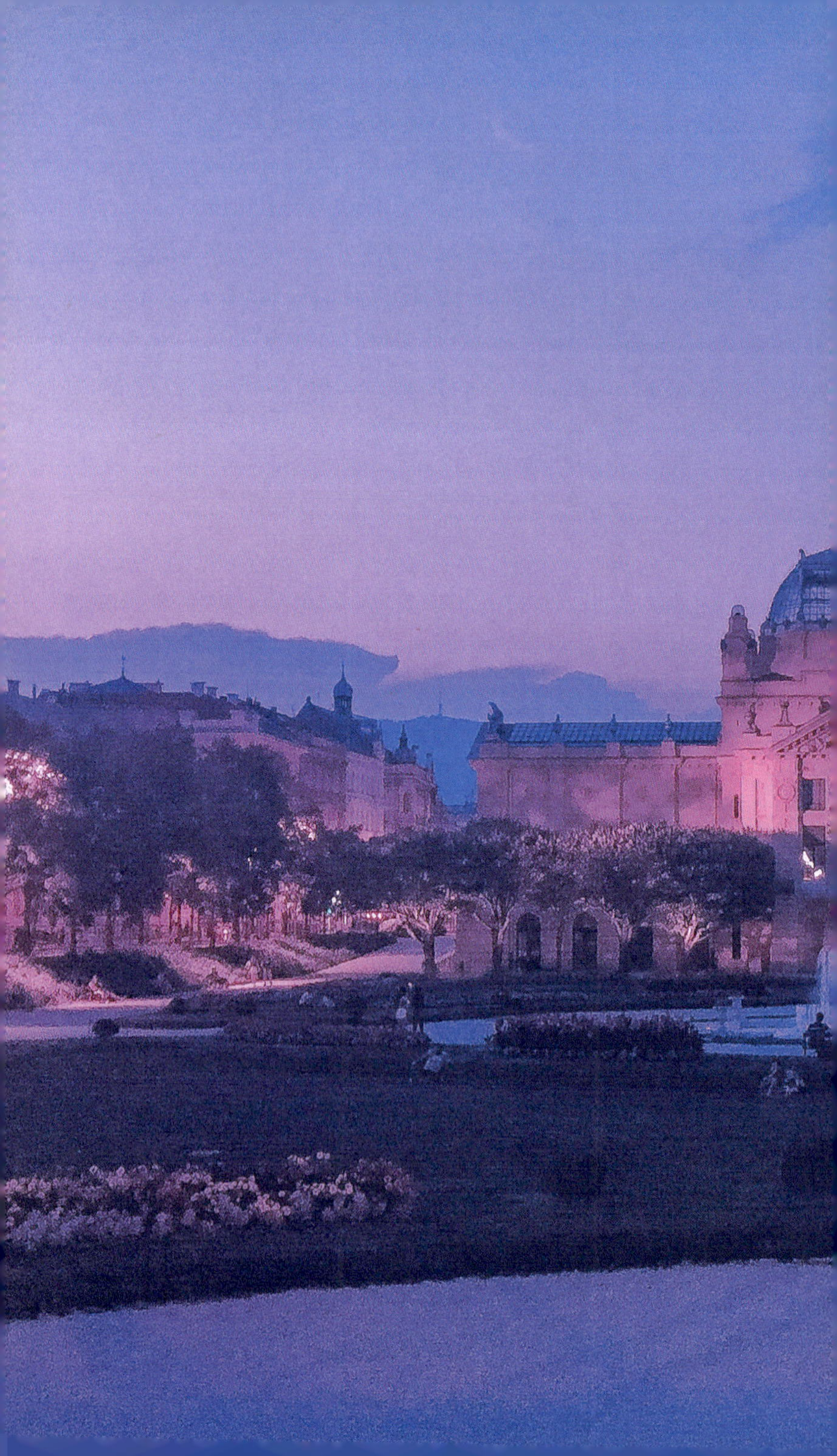

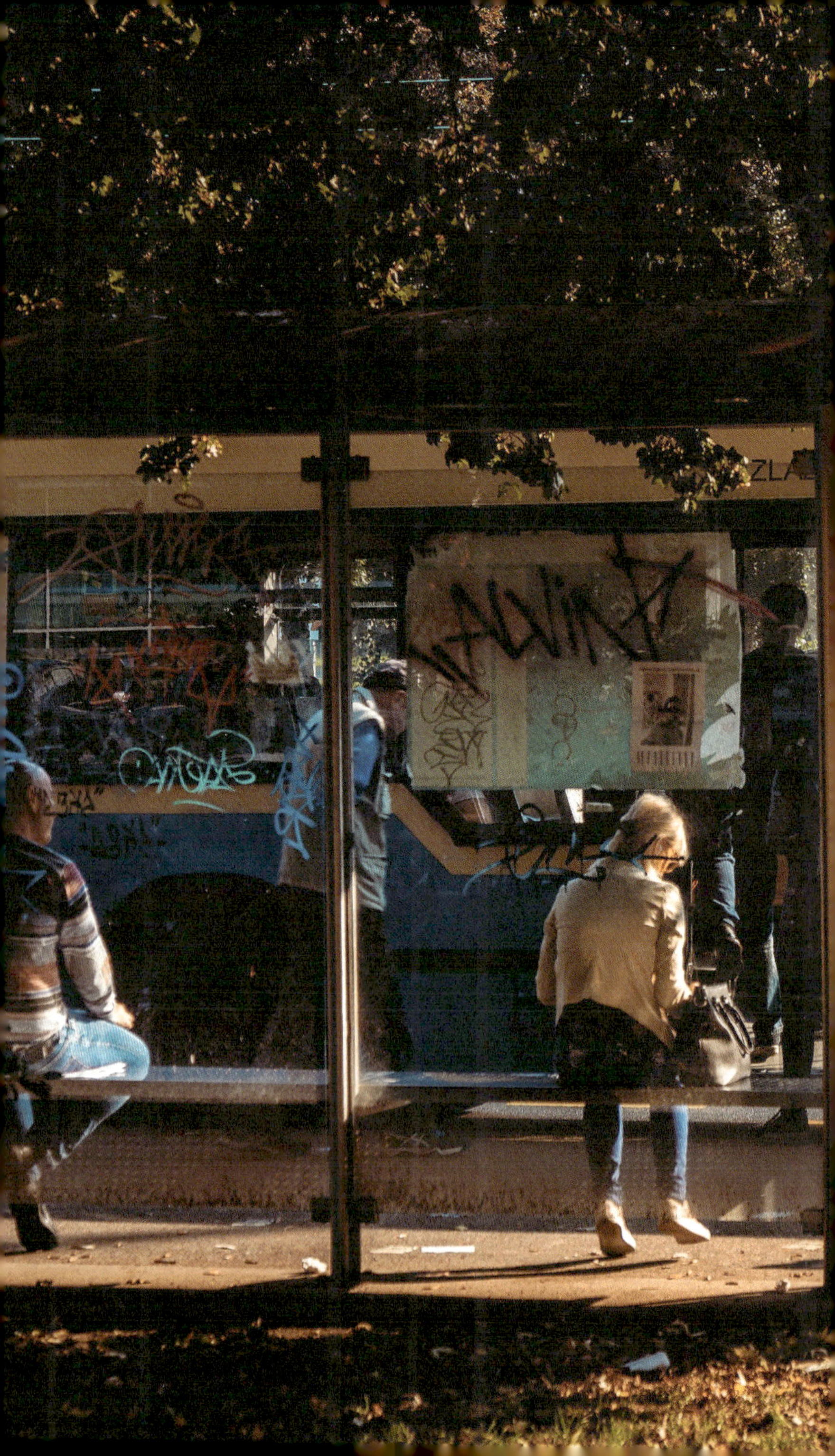

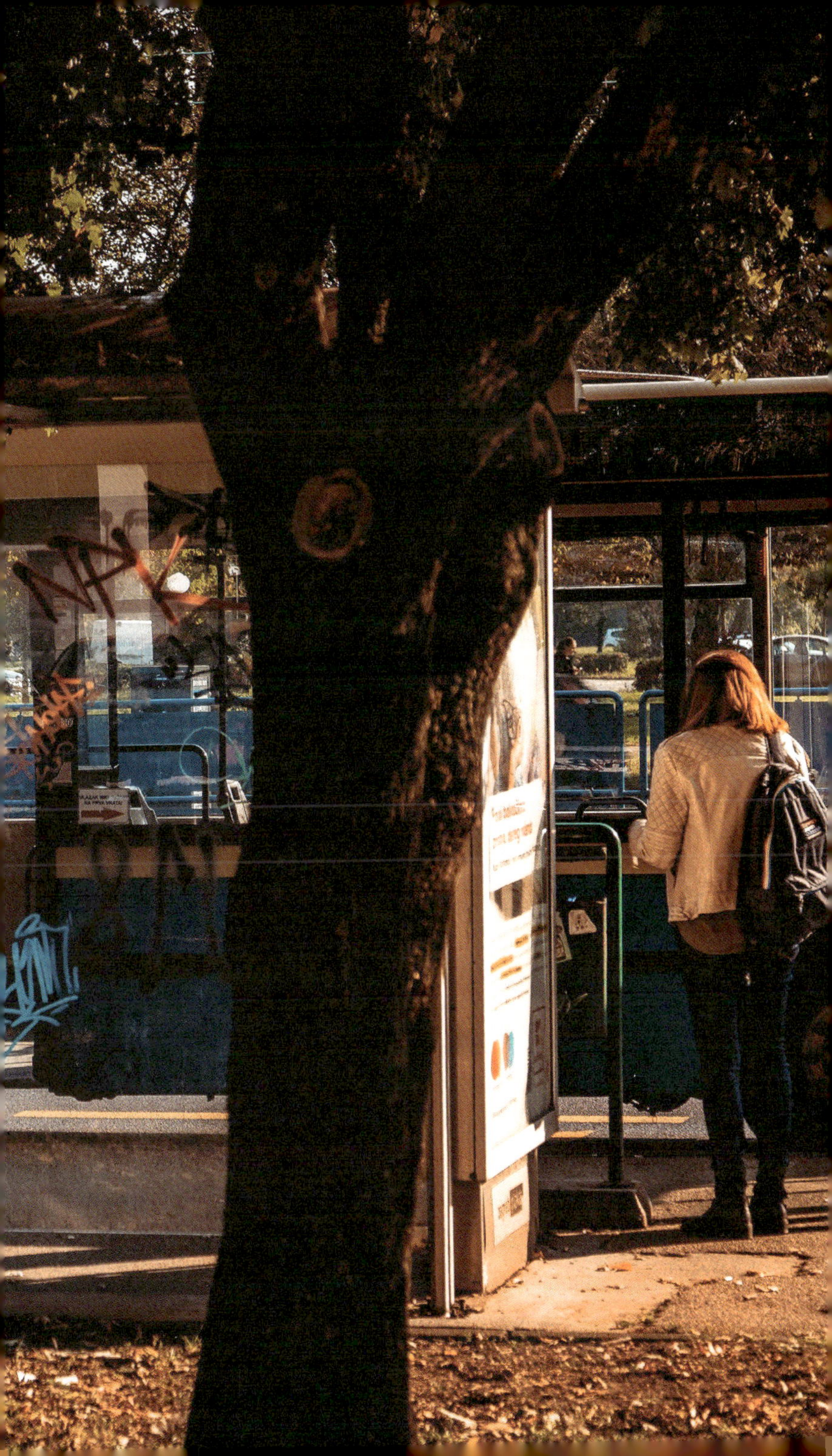

BLAGAJNE ↑ IZLAZ INFORMACIJE BLAGAJNE →

DOLAZAK ODLAZAK

"What you seek is seeking you."
Rumi

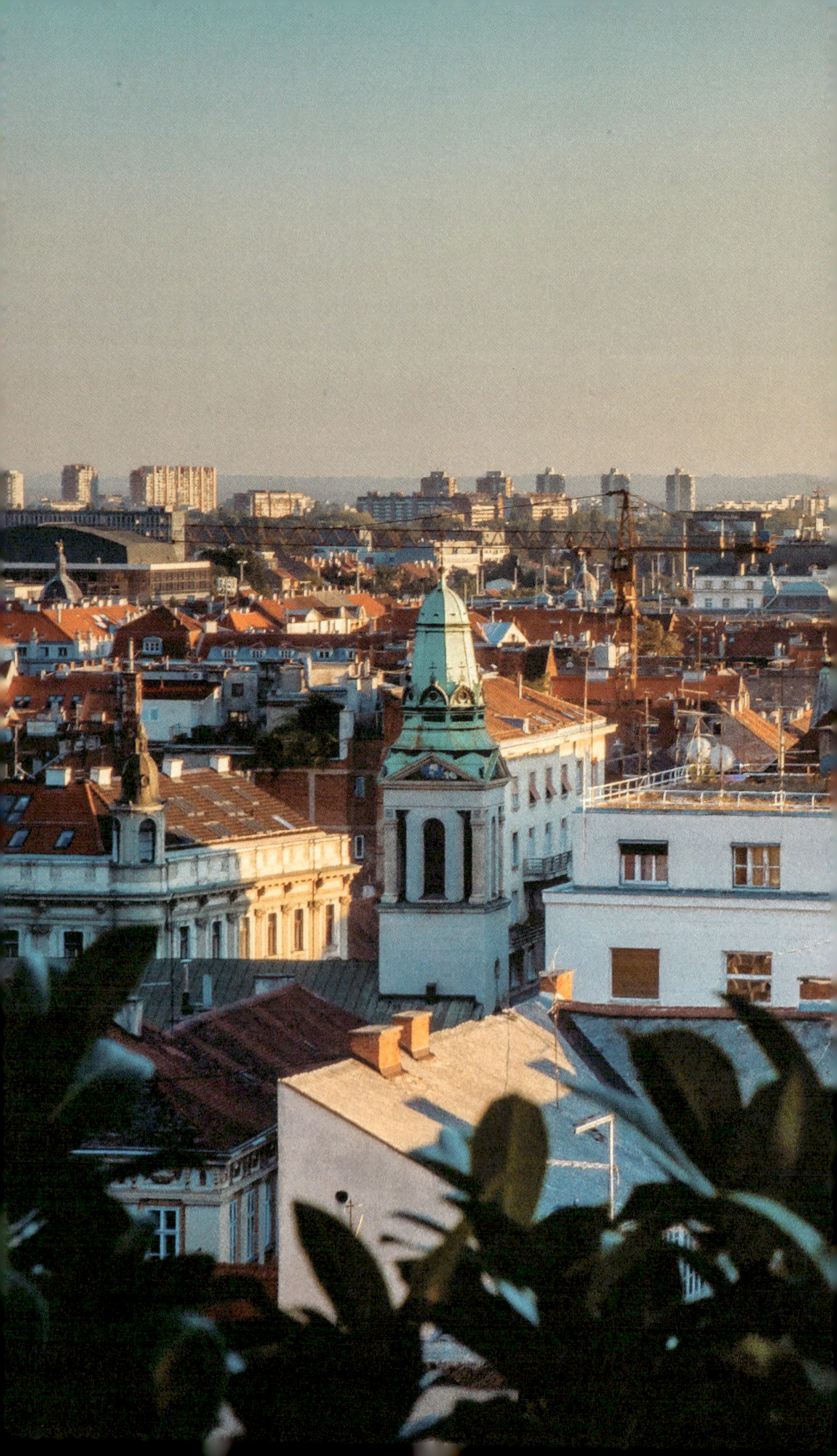

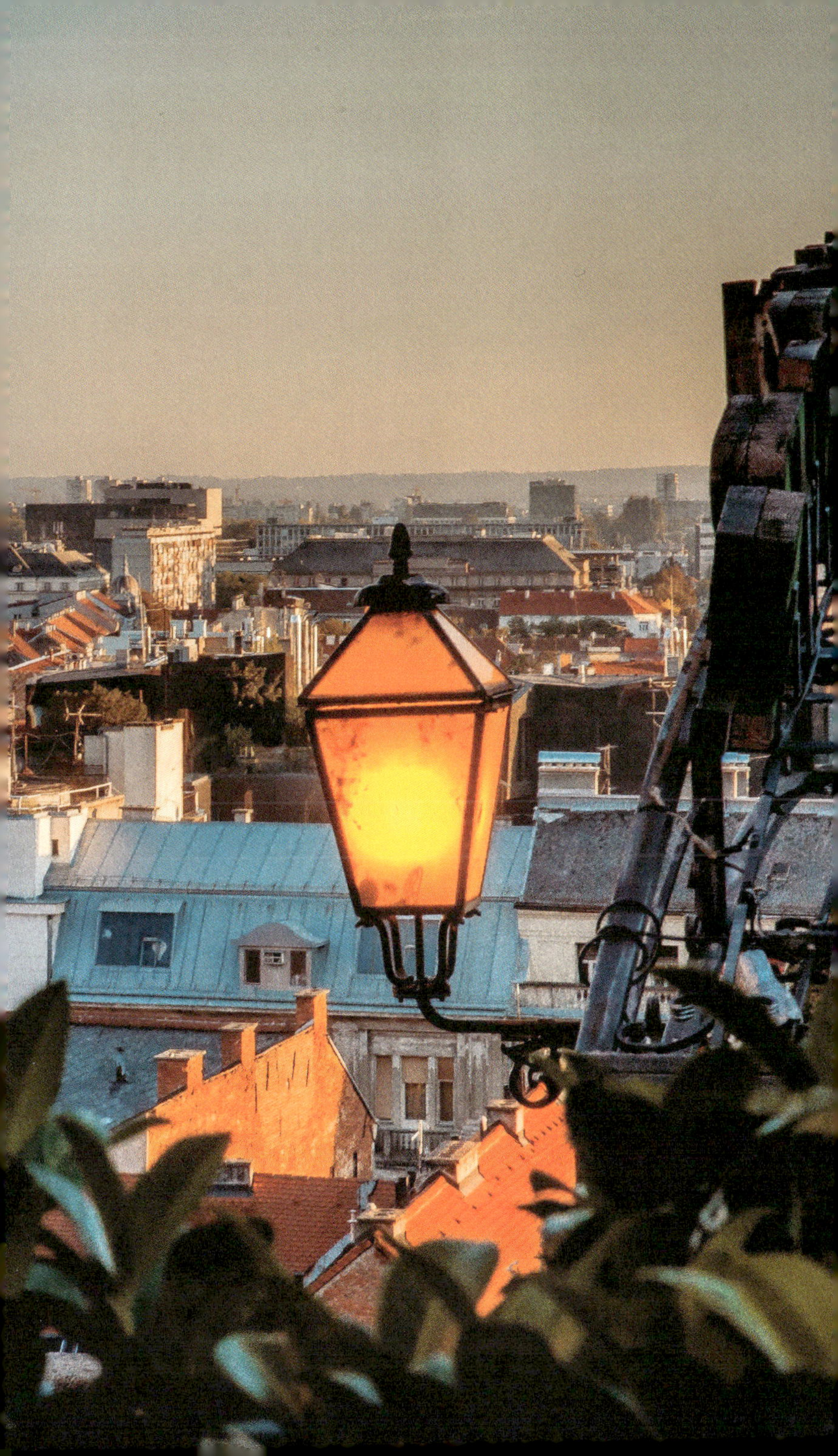

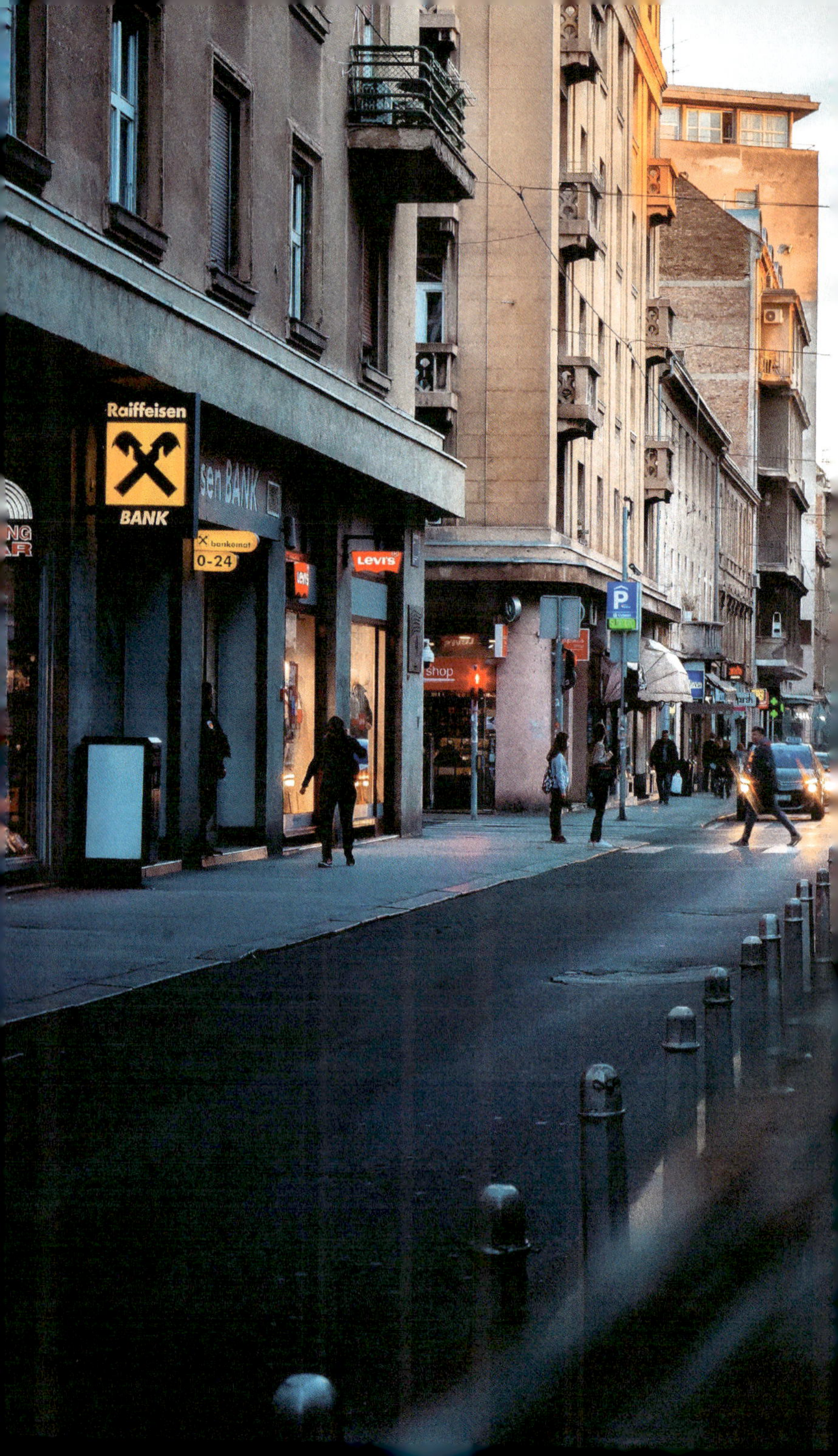
Raiffeisen
BANK
sen BANK
bankomat
0-24
Levi's
shop
P

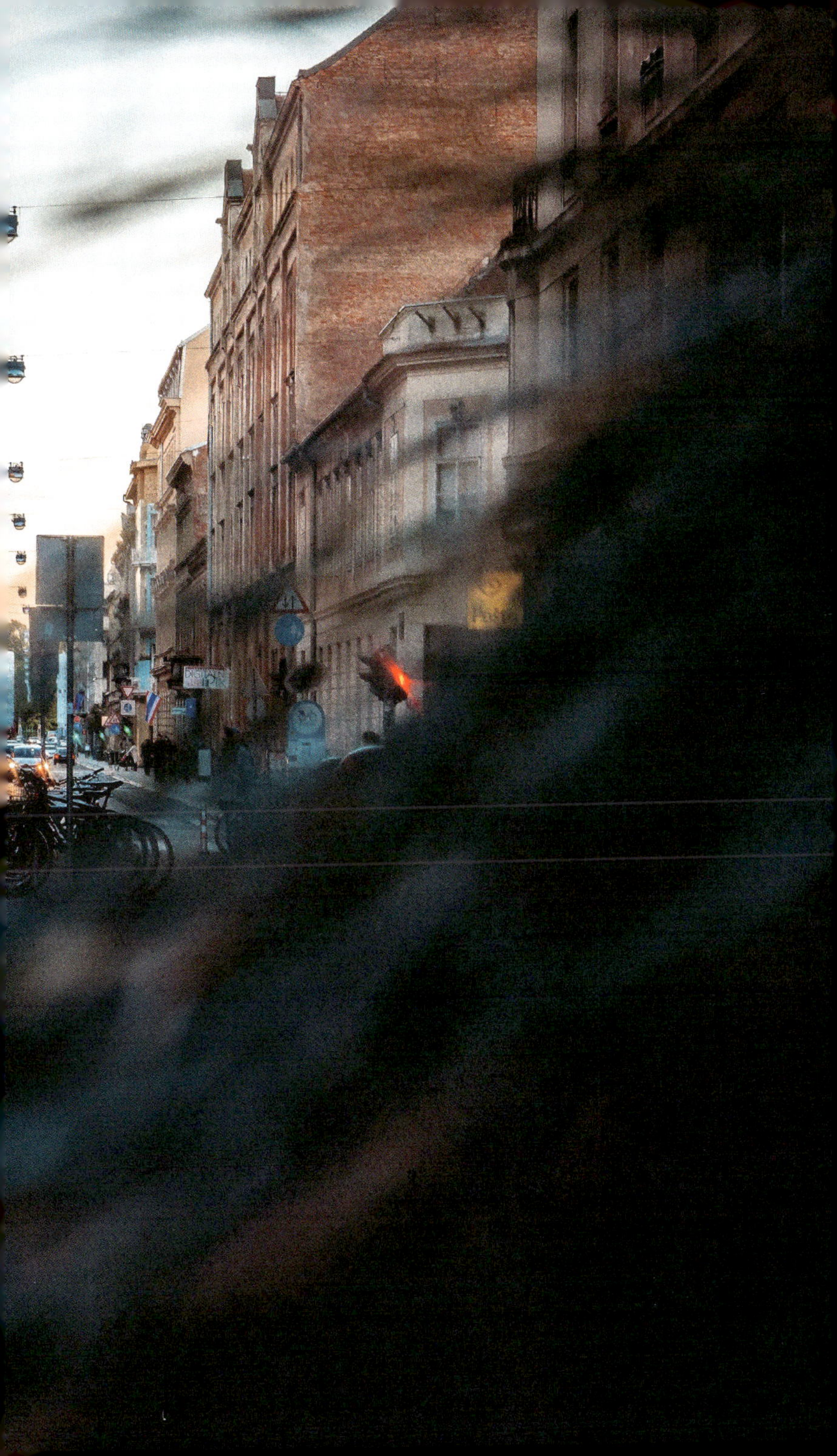

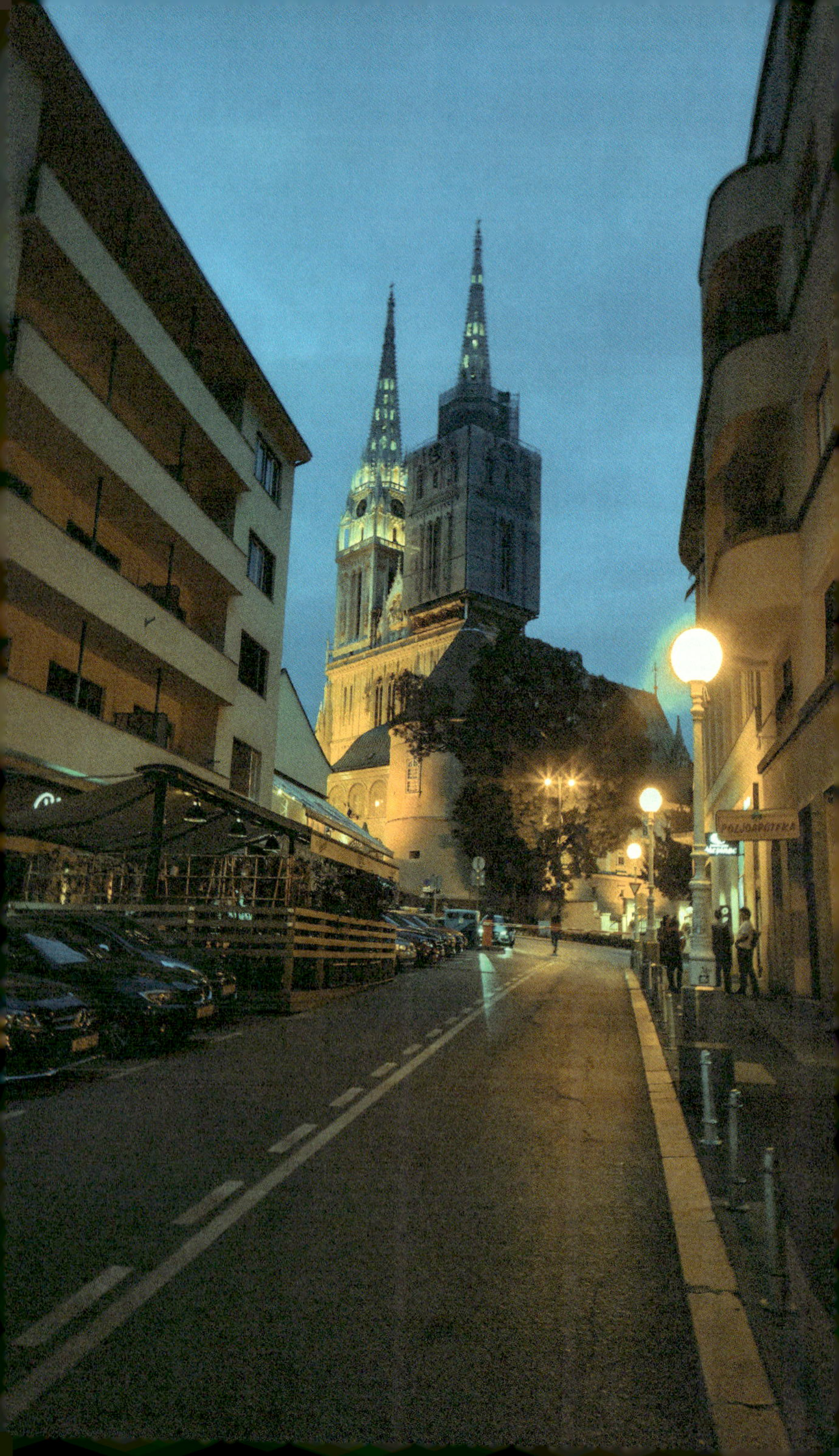

"He lay in bed, waiting for life to come to him. Since life was not to be seen, he realised he had to get up and look for it himself."

Thomas Mann

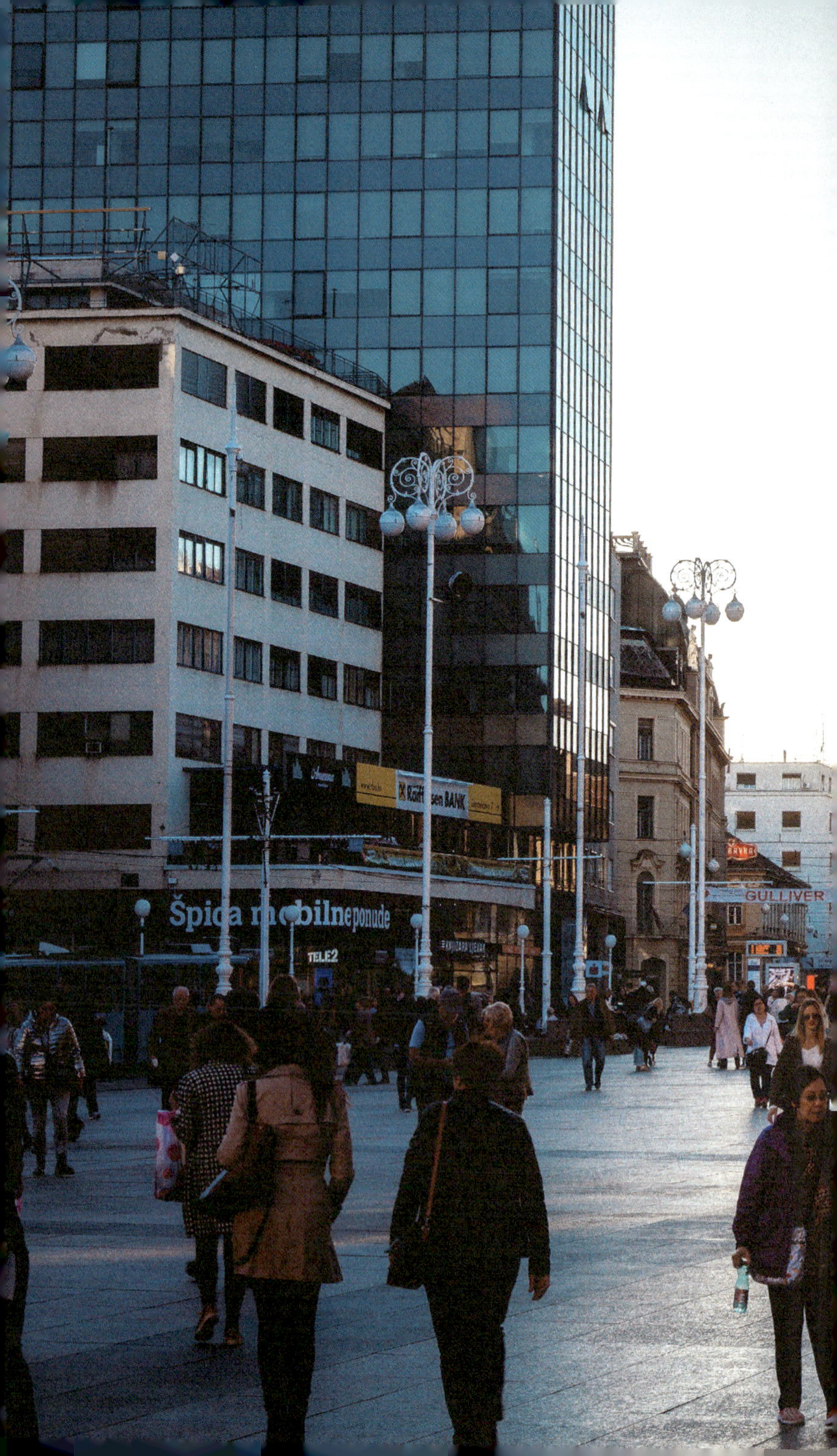
BANK
TELE2
GULLIVER

Internorm
hoco-stabil.hr
otpbanka
VIŠE OD 23 GODINE ISKUSTVA
PRIJEVODI
SUDSKI TUMAČI
TEČAJEVI

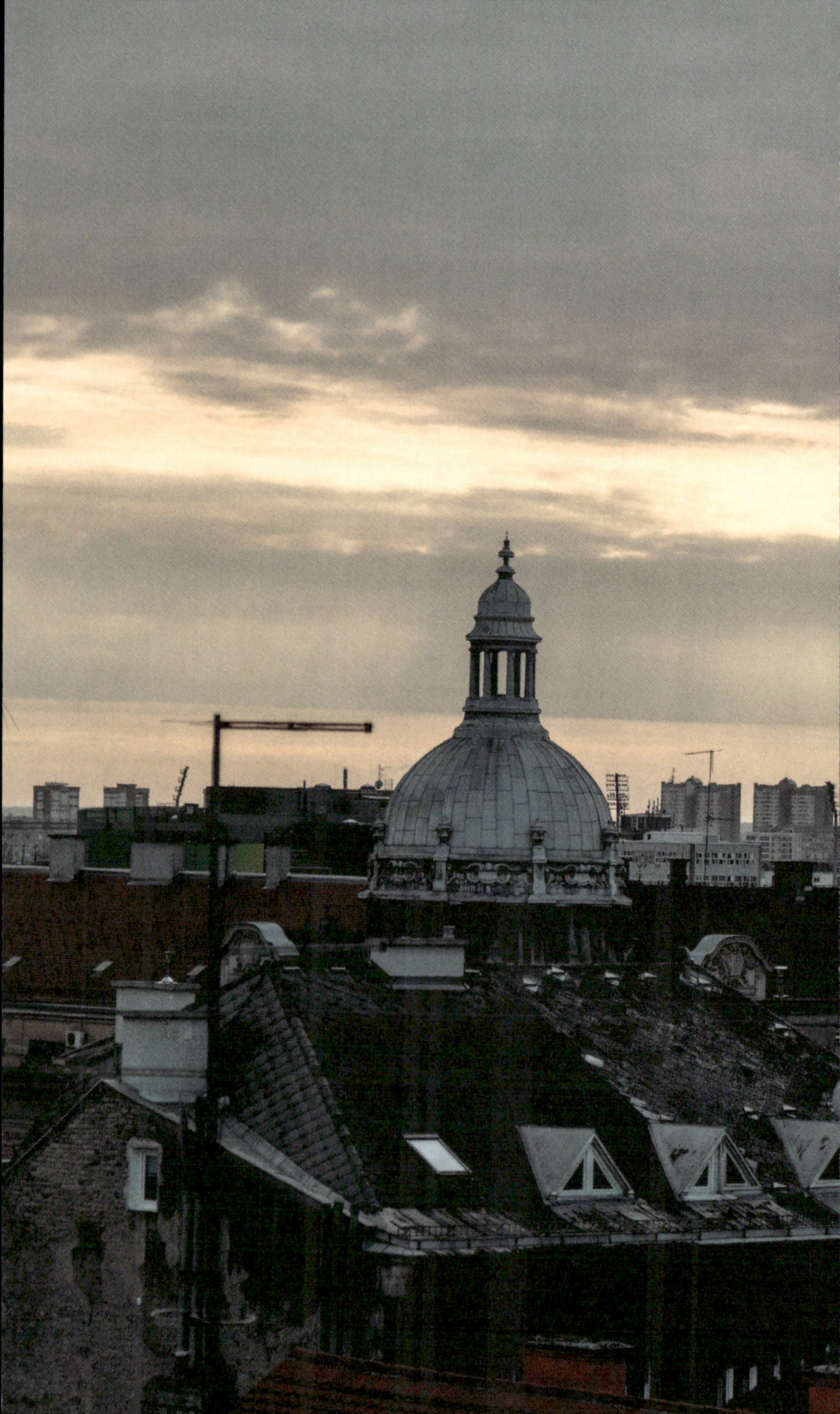

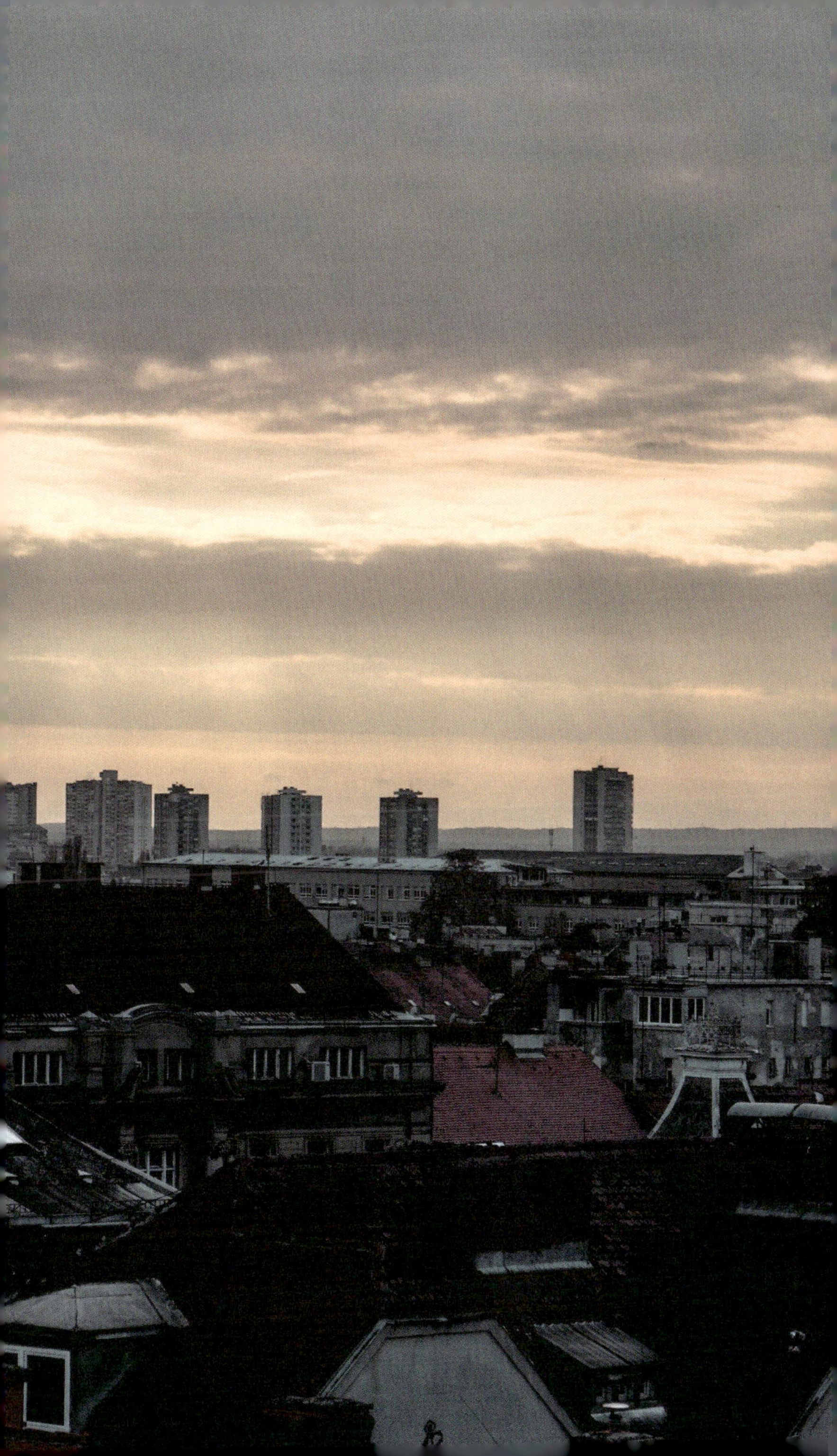

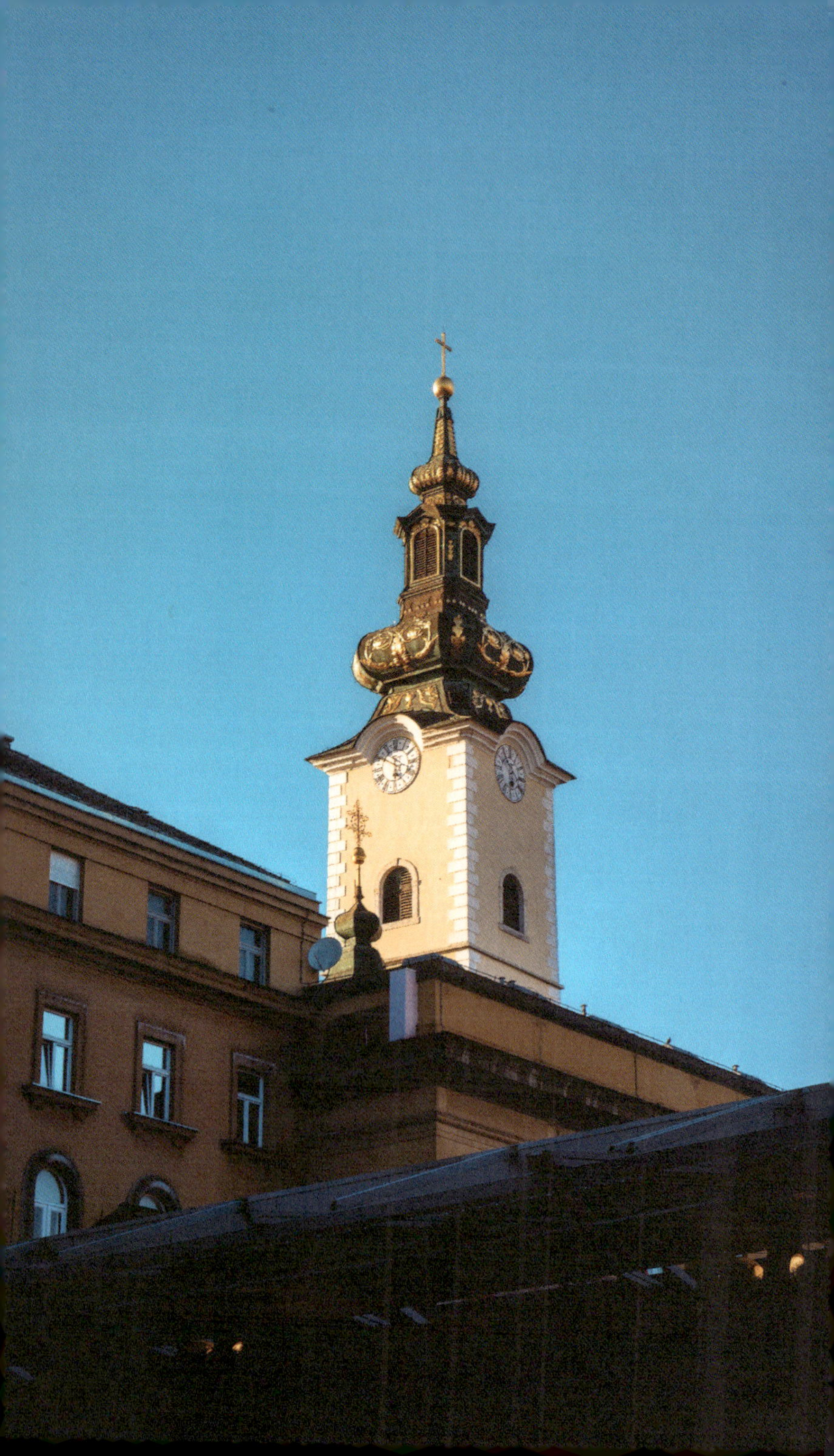

"The picture that you took with your camera is the imagination you want to create with reality."
Scott Lorenzo

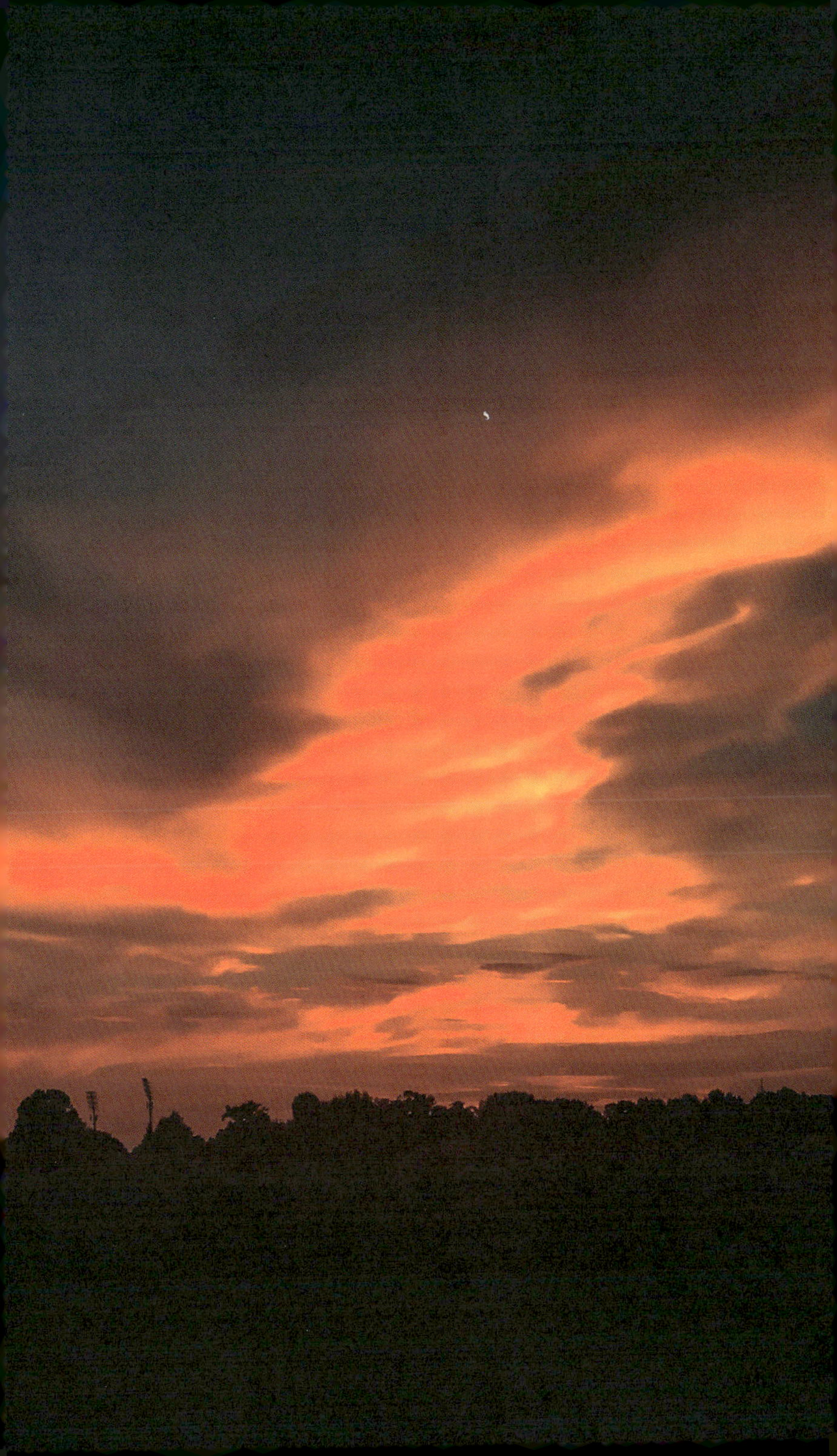

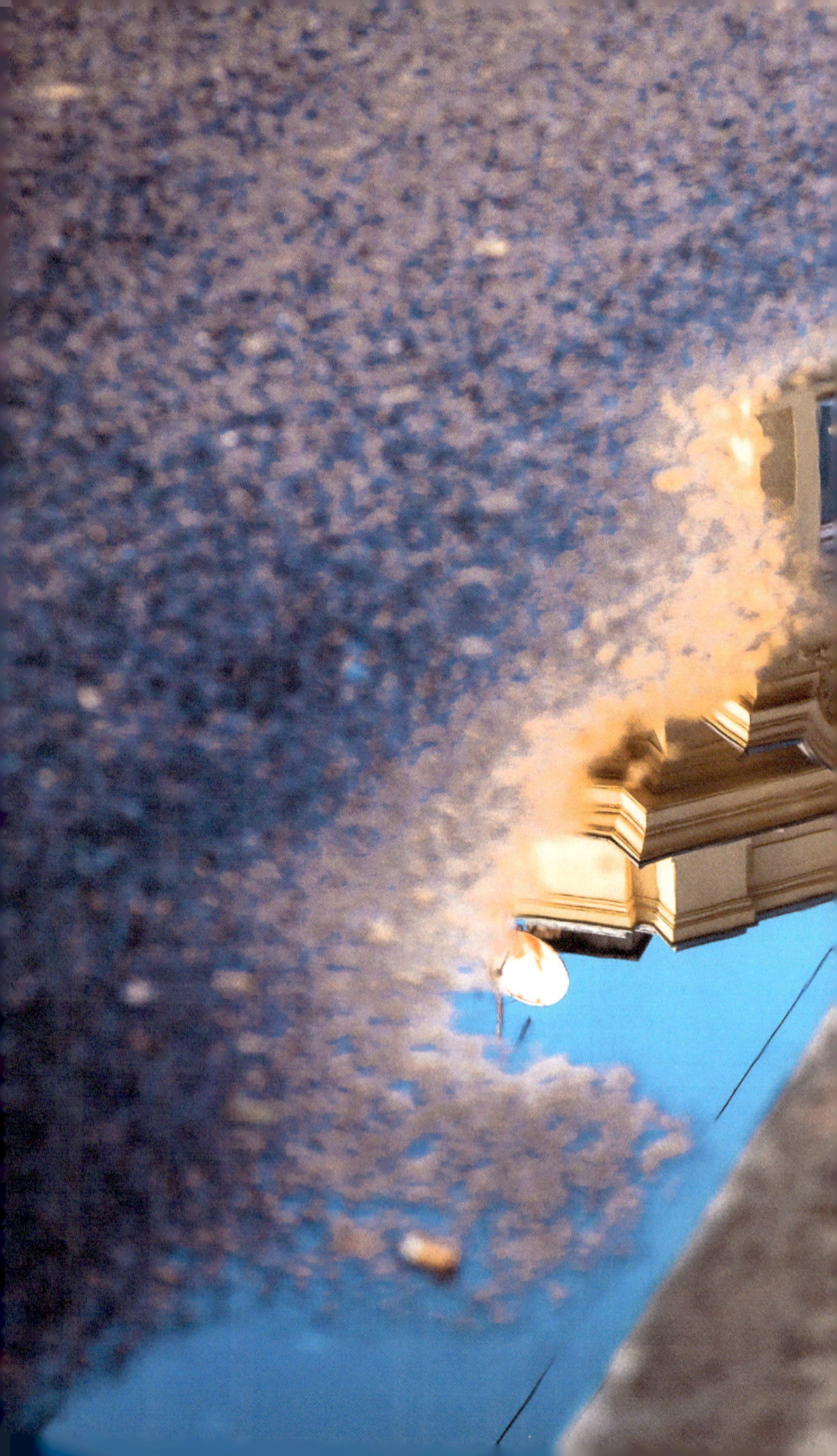

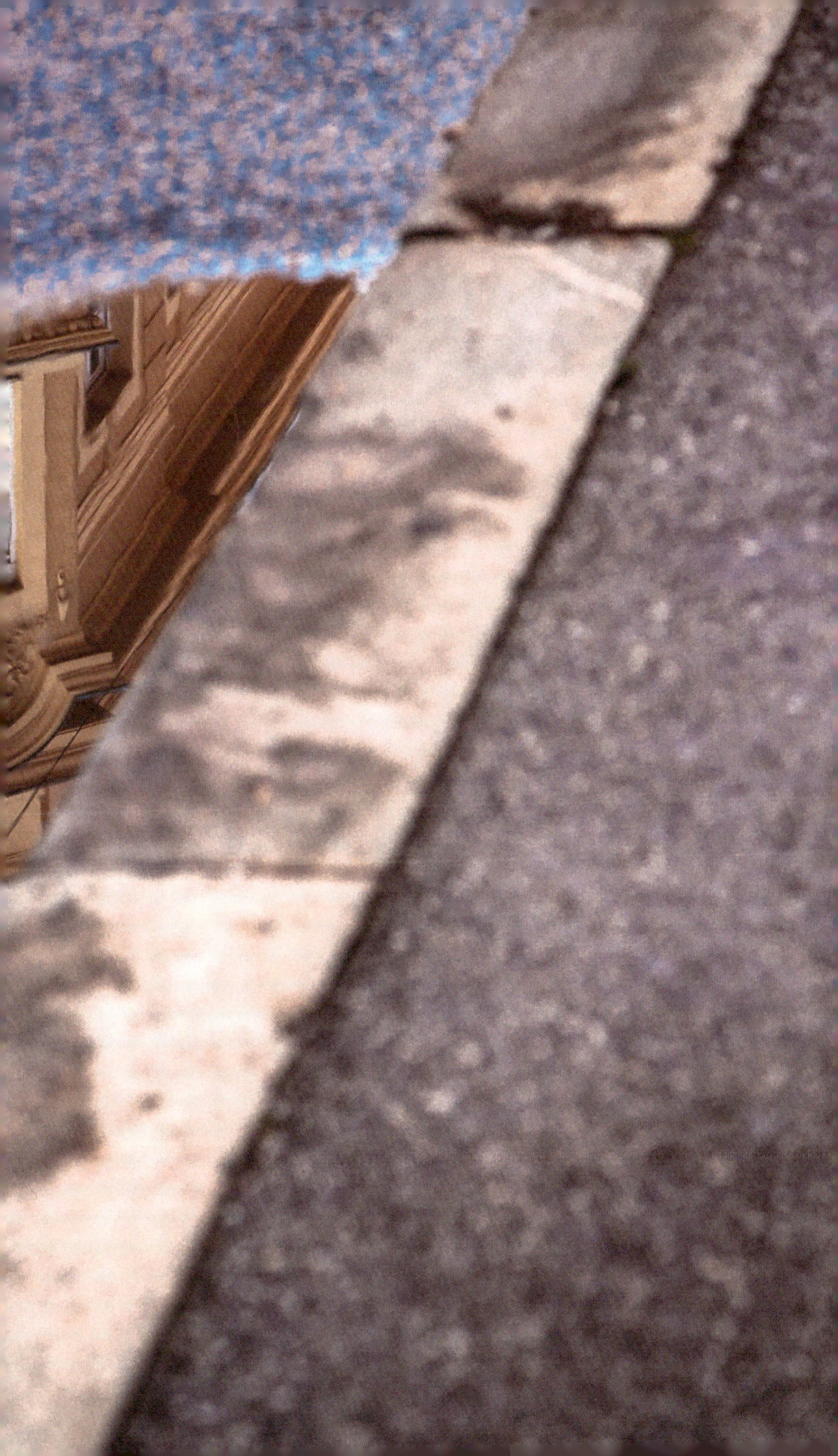

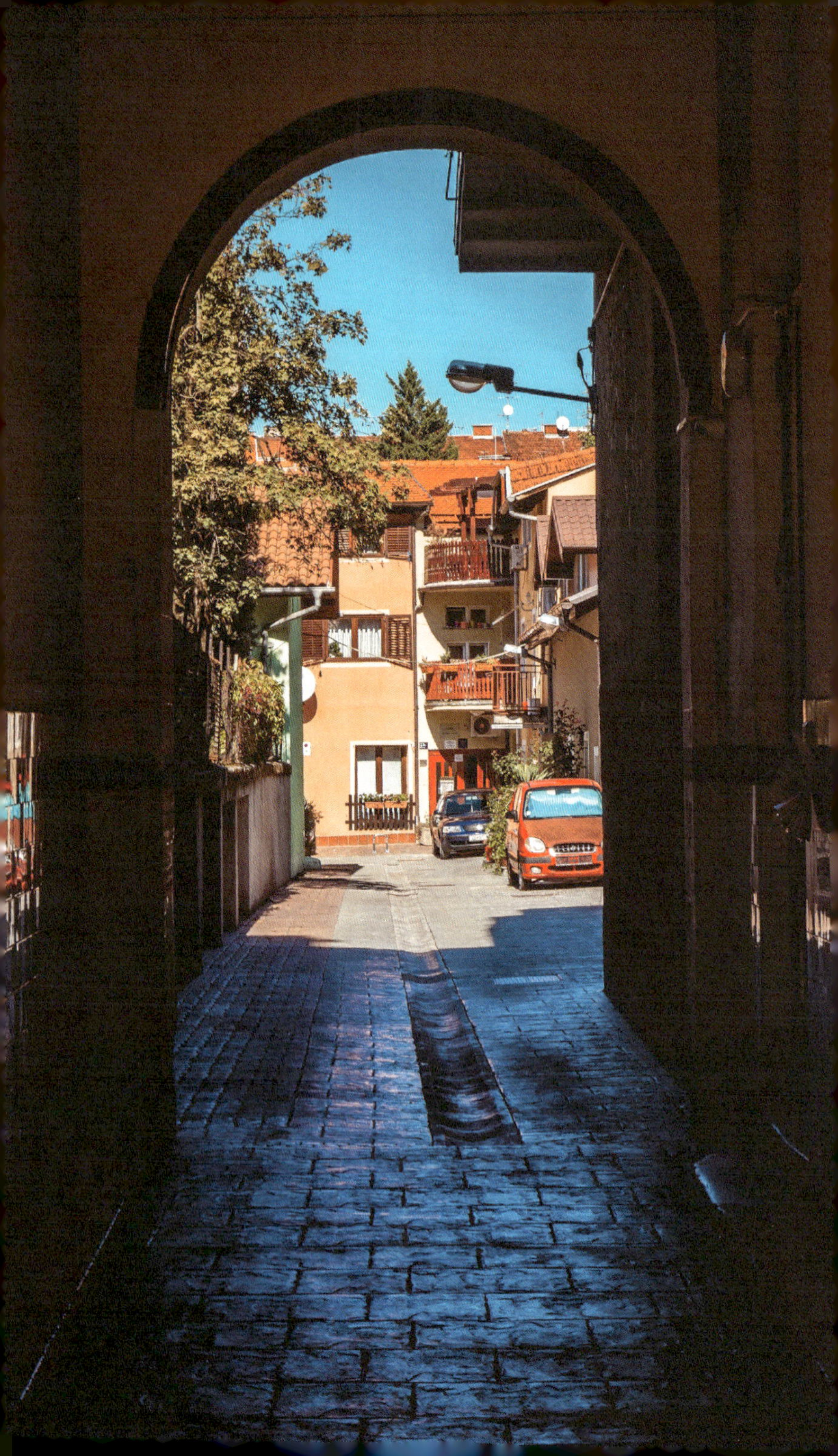

"Distance is like the future: as soon as we rush towards it, it becomes our present – same as it had been and we find ourselves in our own destitution again."
Goethe

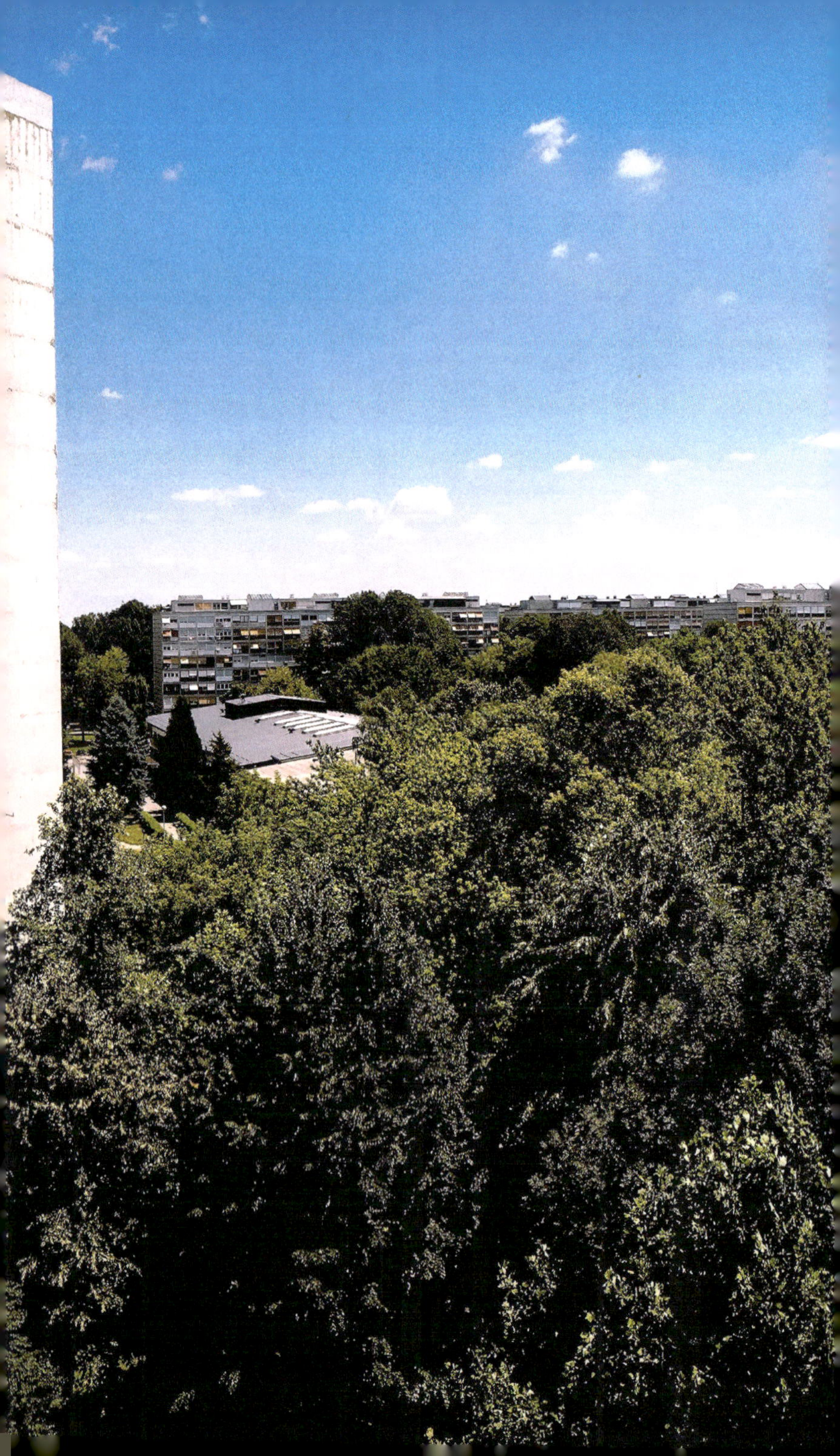

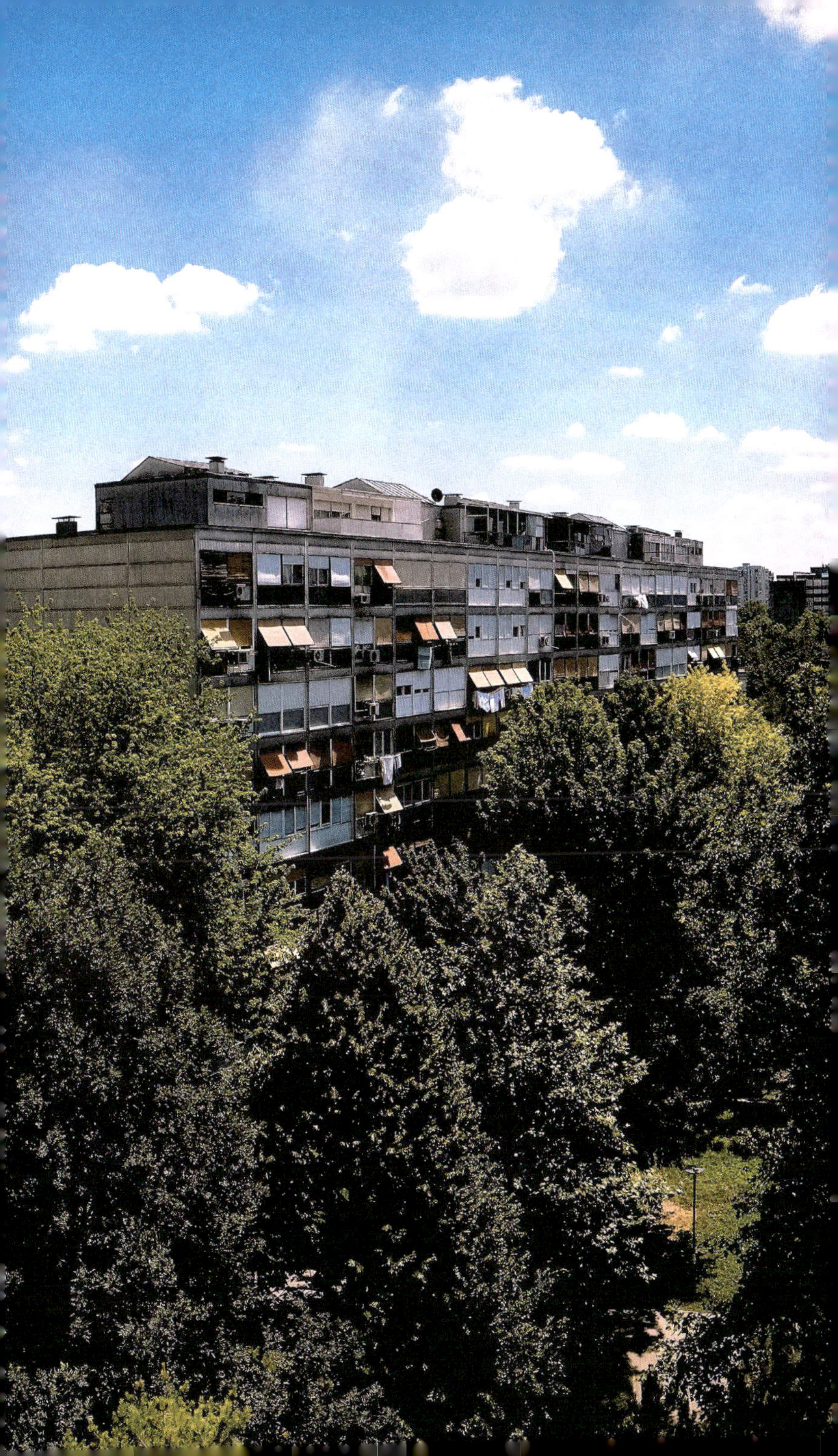

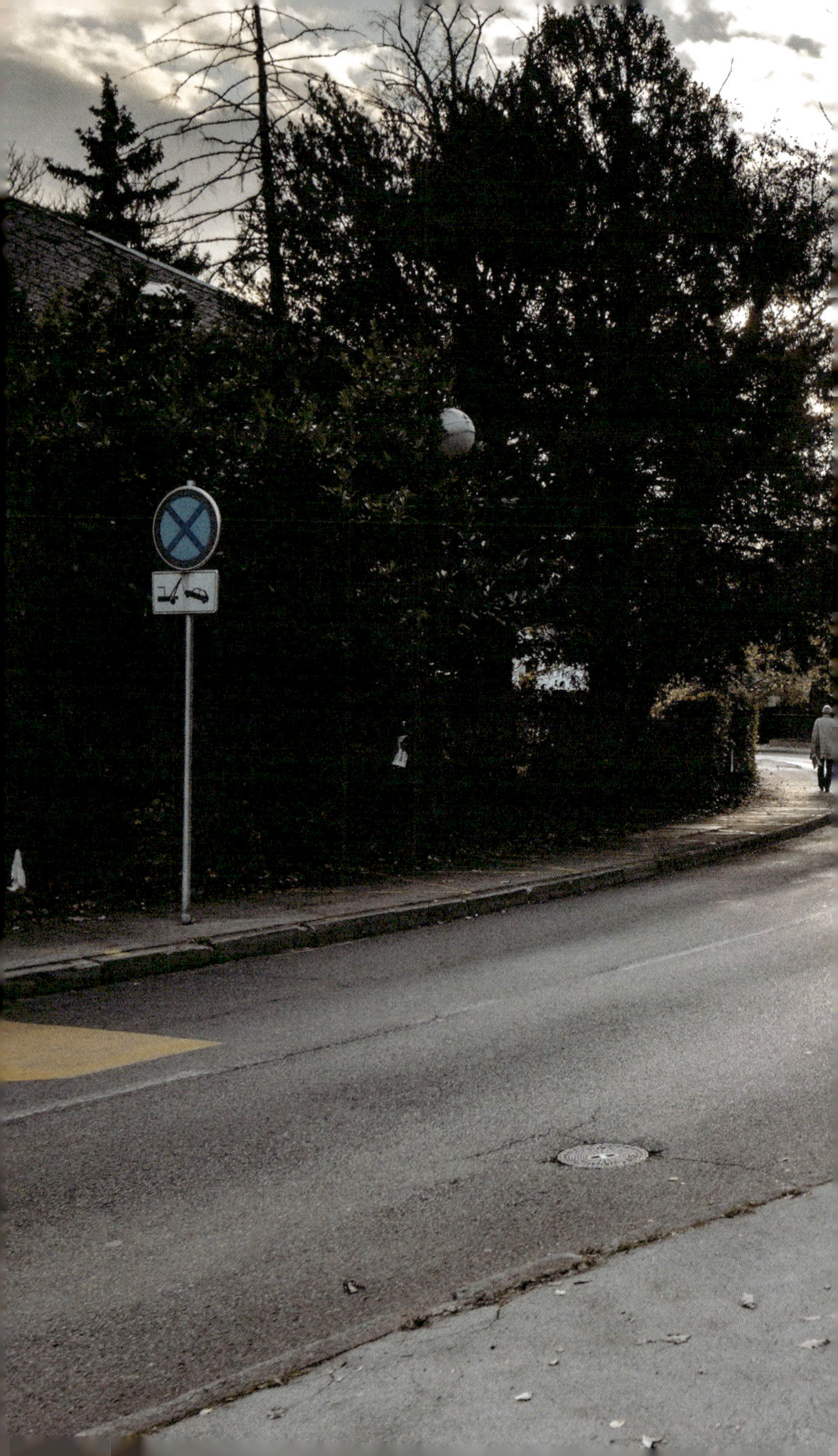

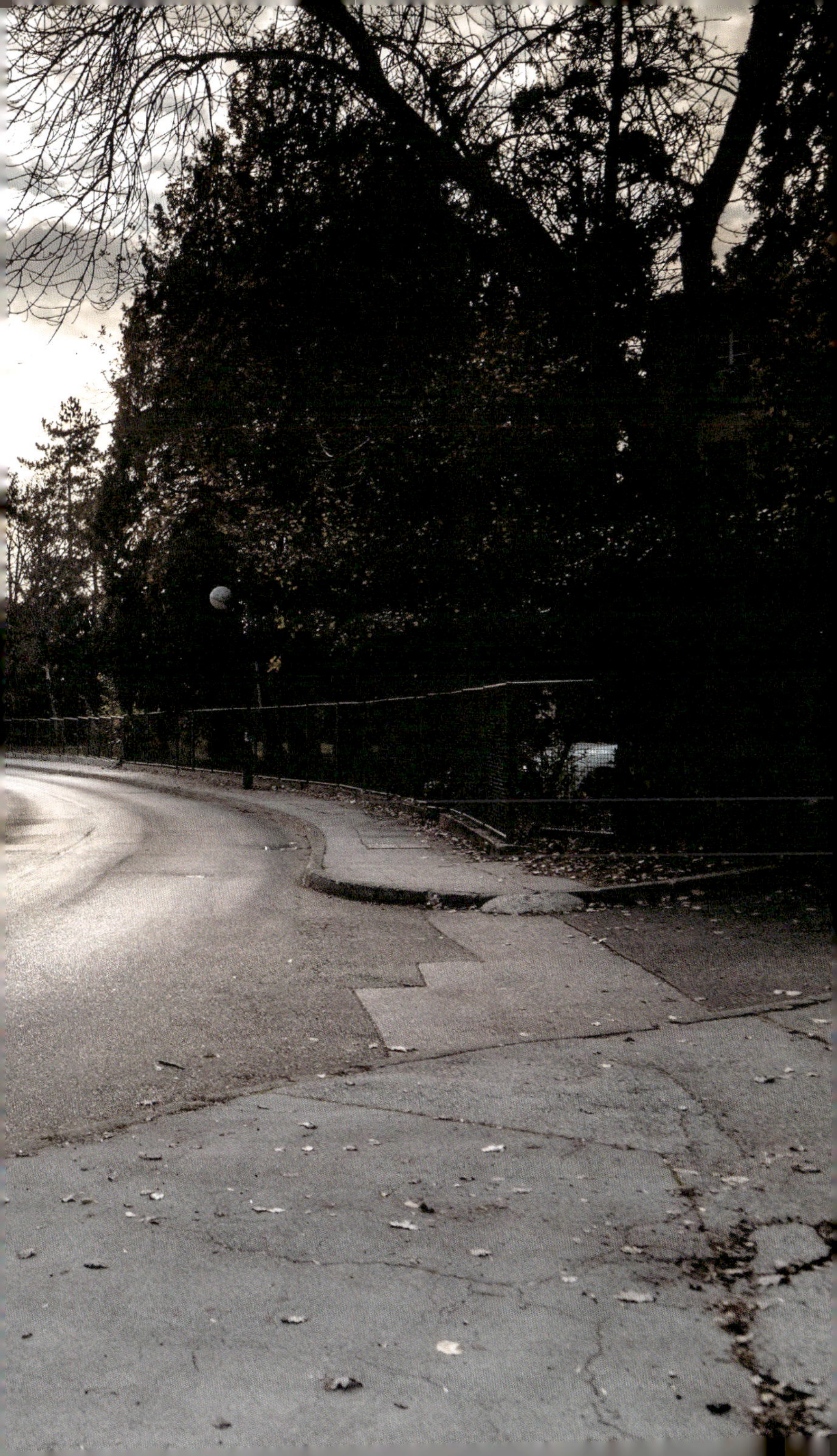

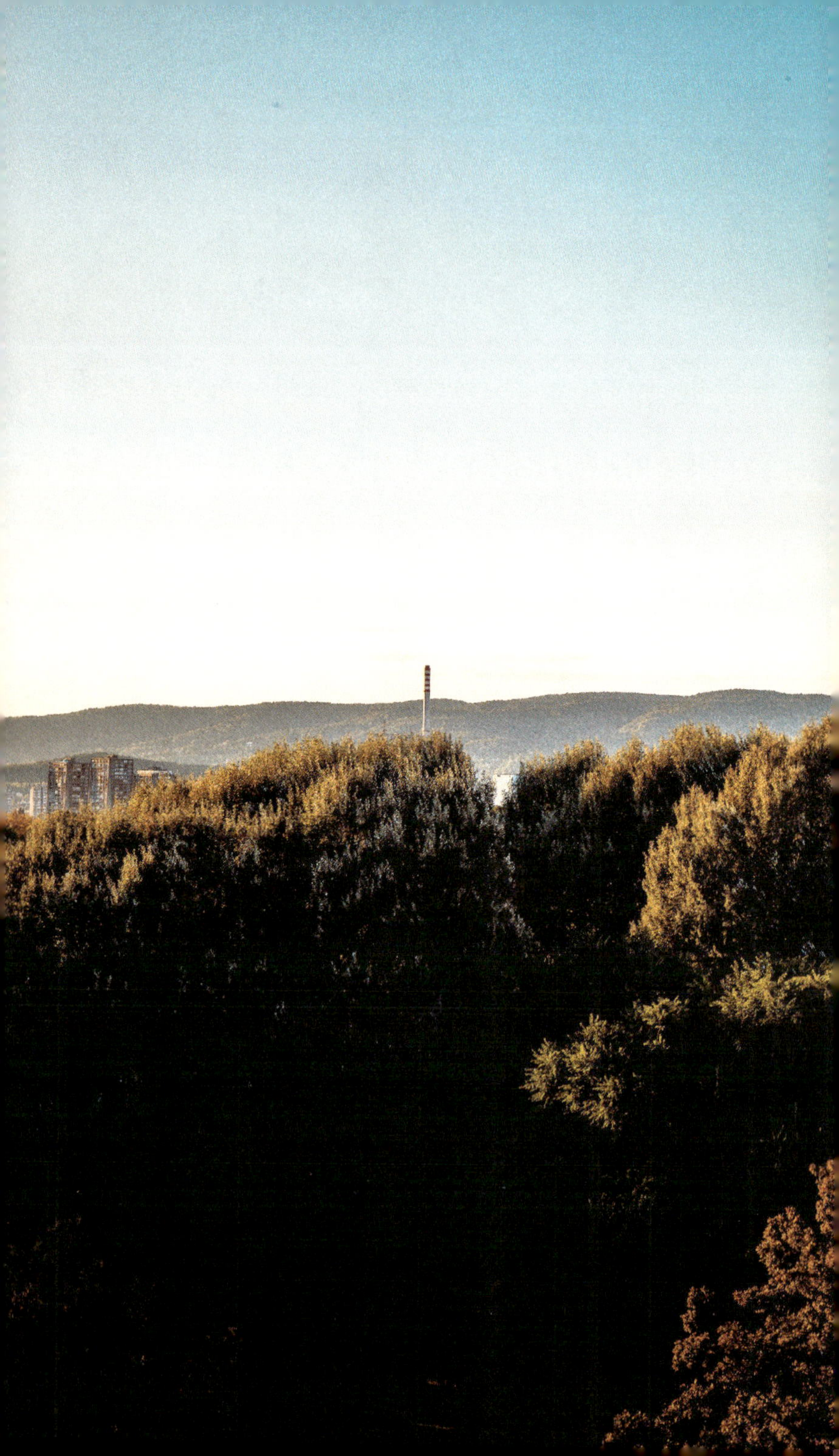

"Which of my photographs is my favorite? The one I'm going to take tomorrow."
Imogen Cunningham

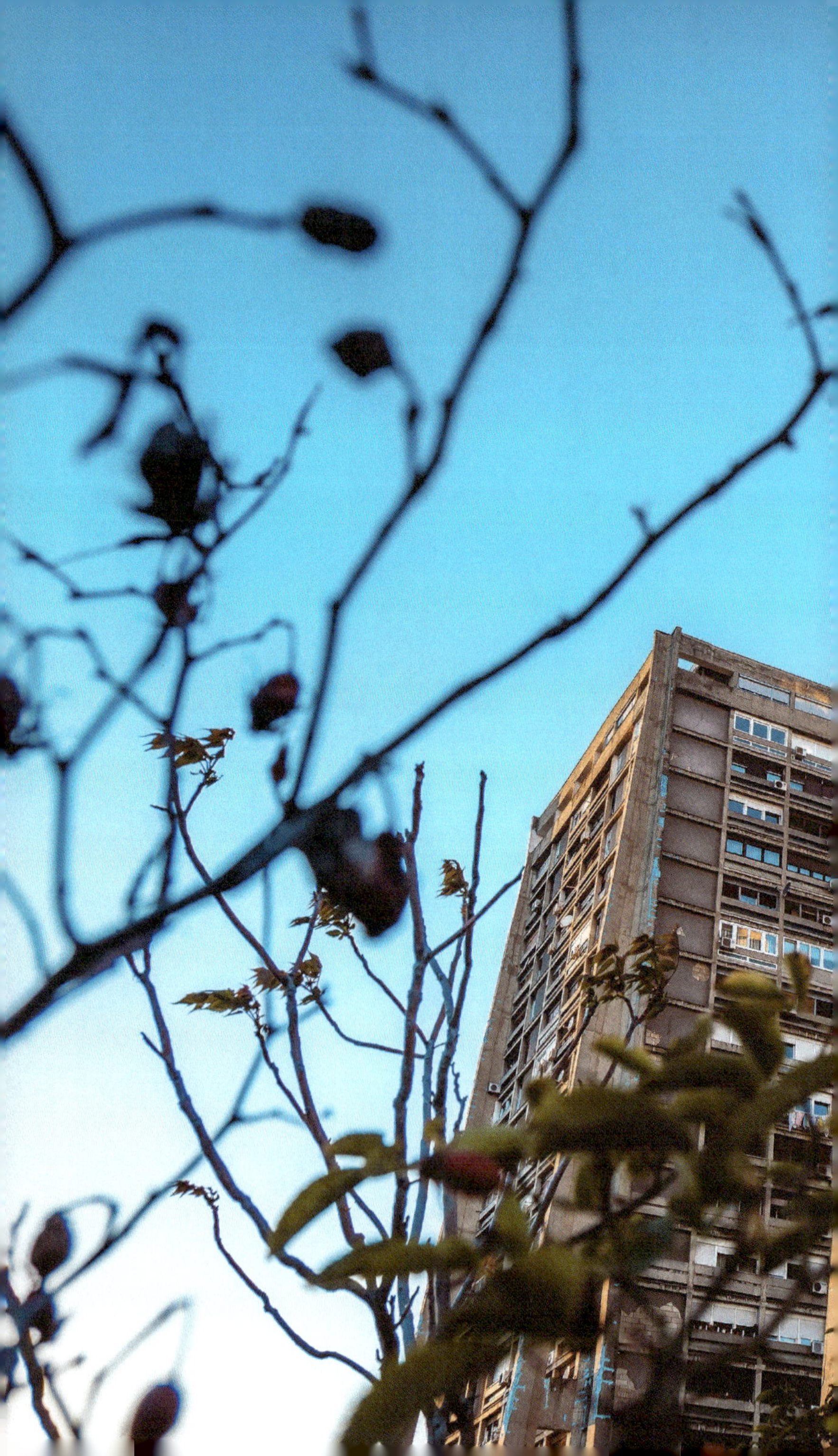

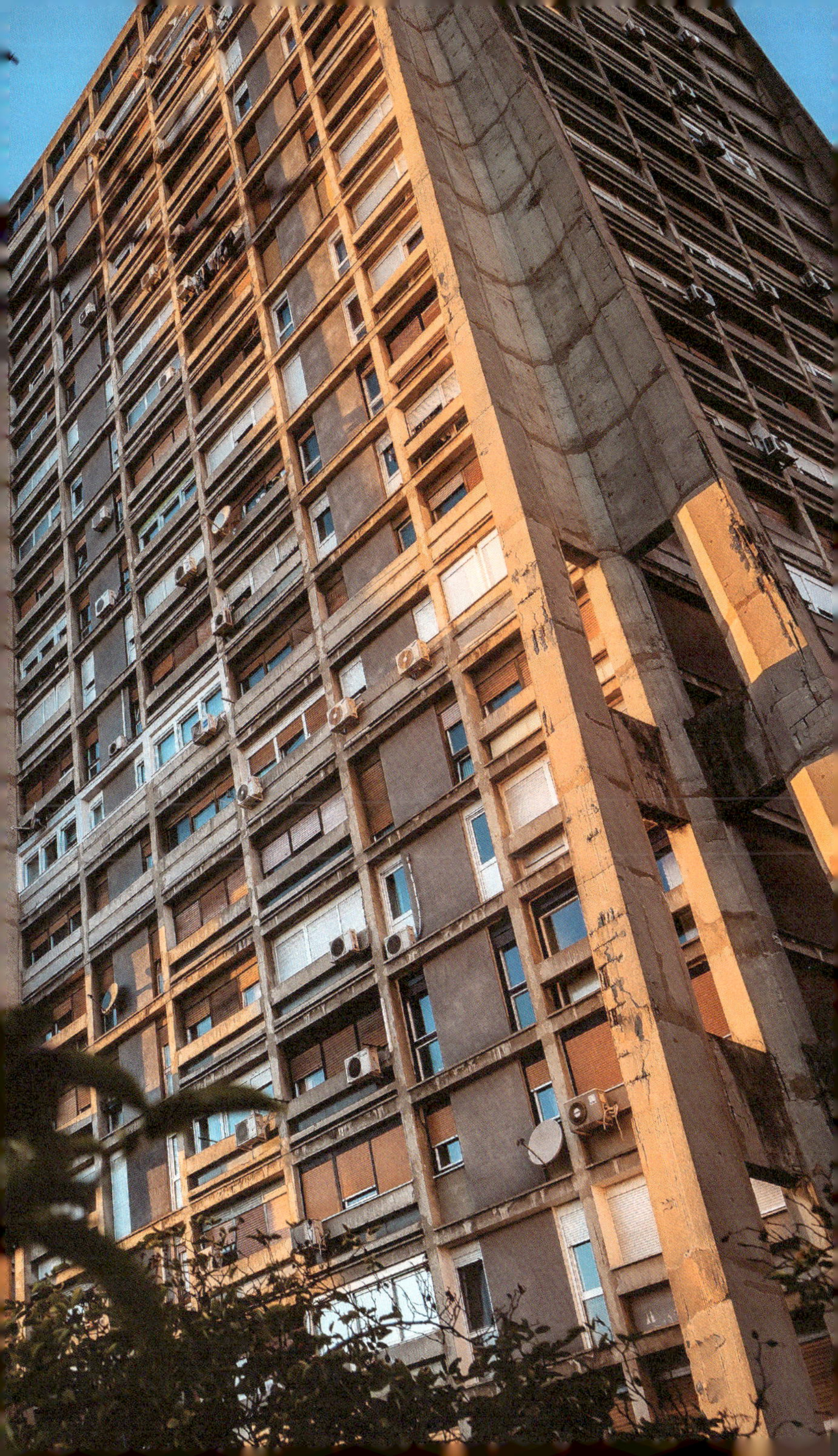

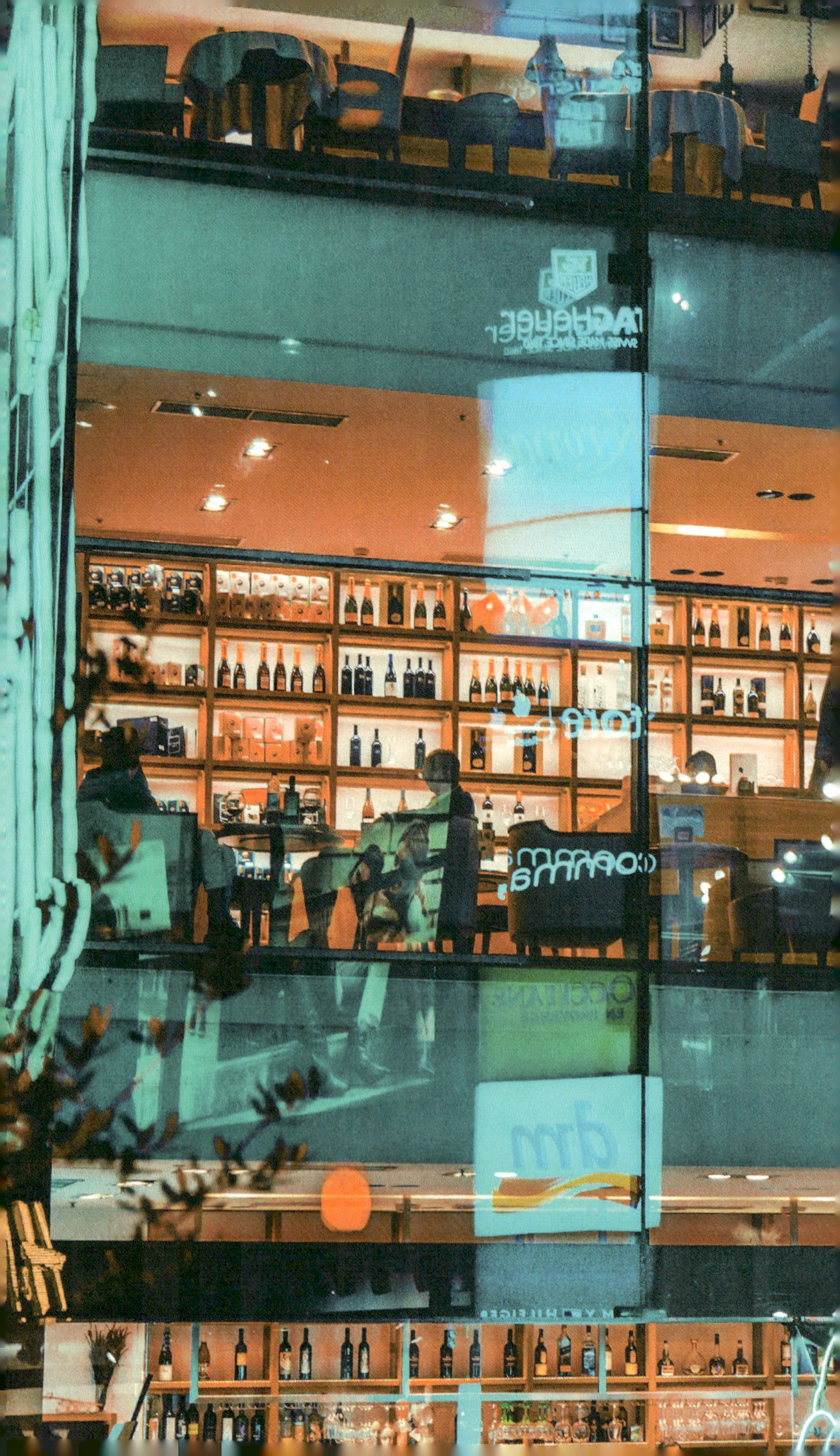

BAR &

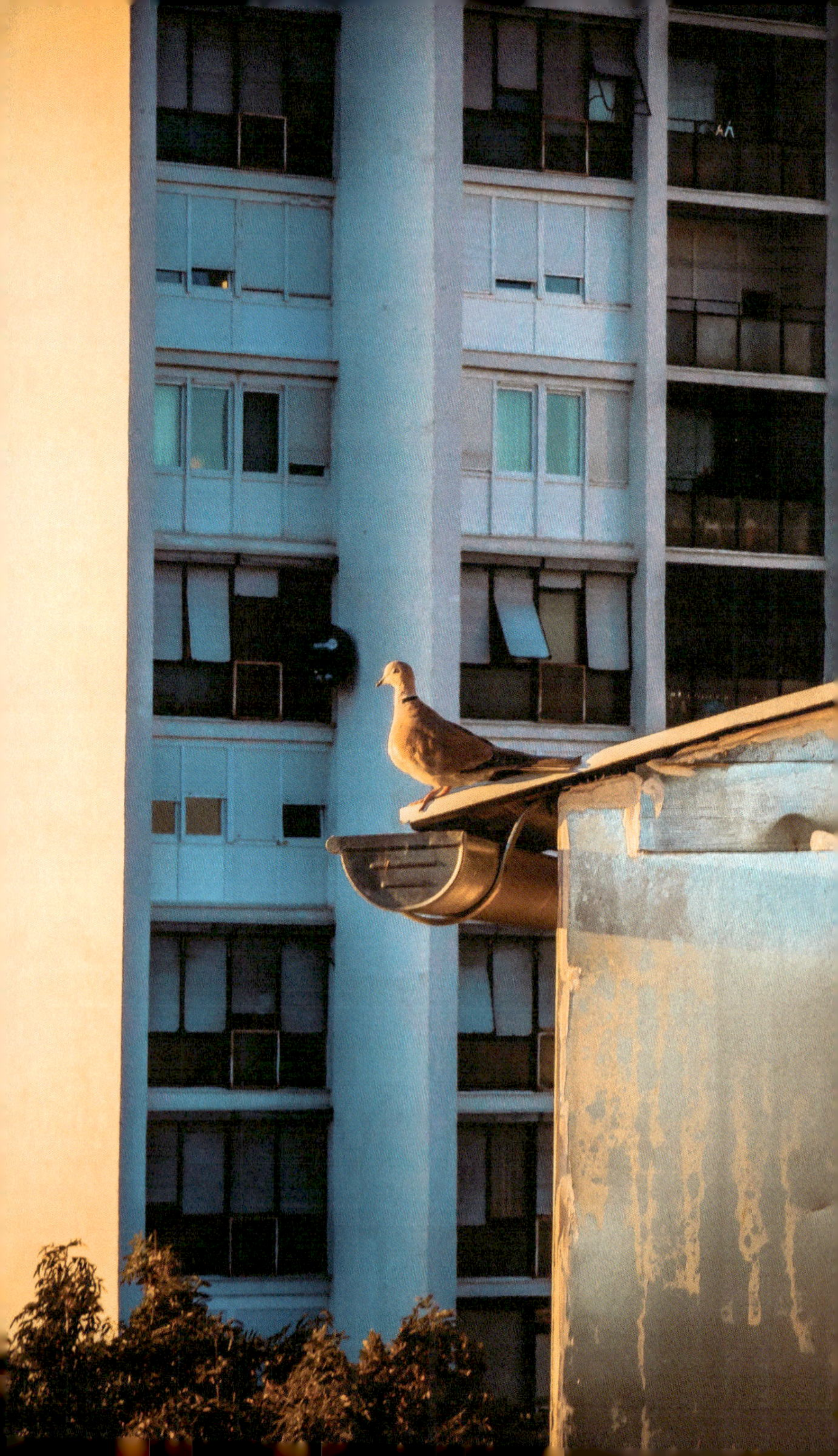

"We are what our thoughts have made us; so take care about what you think. Words are secondary. Thoughts live; they travel far."
Swami Vivekananda

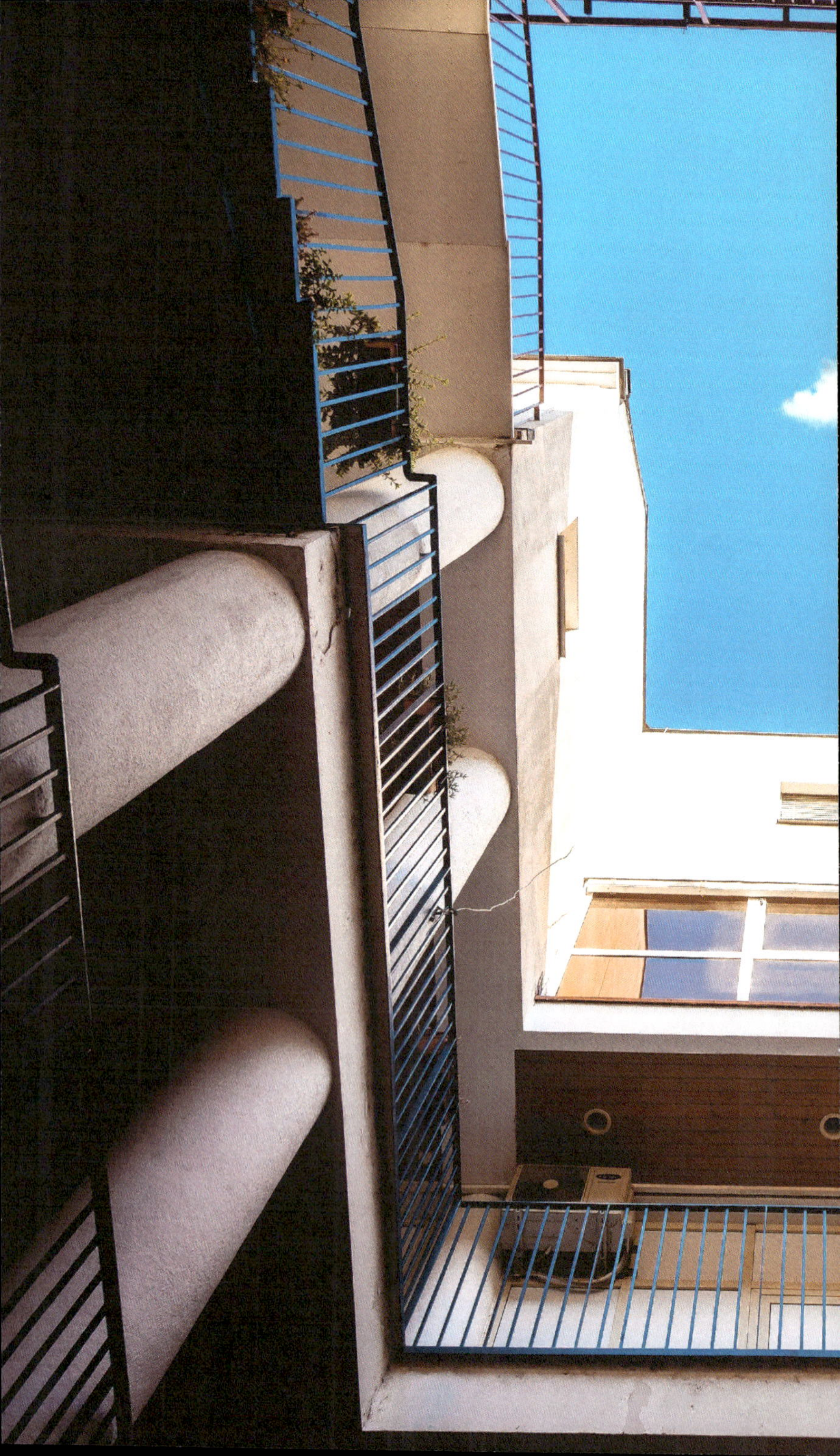

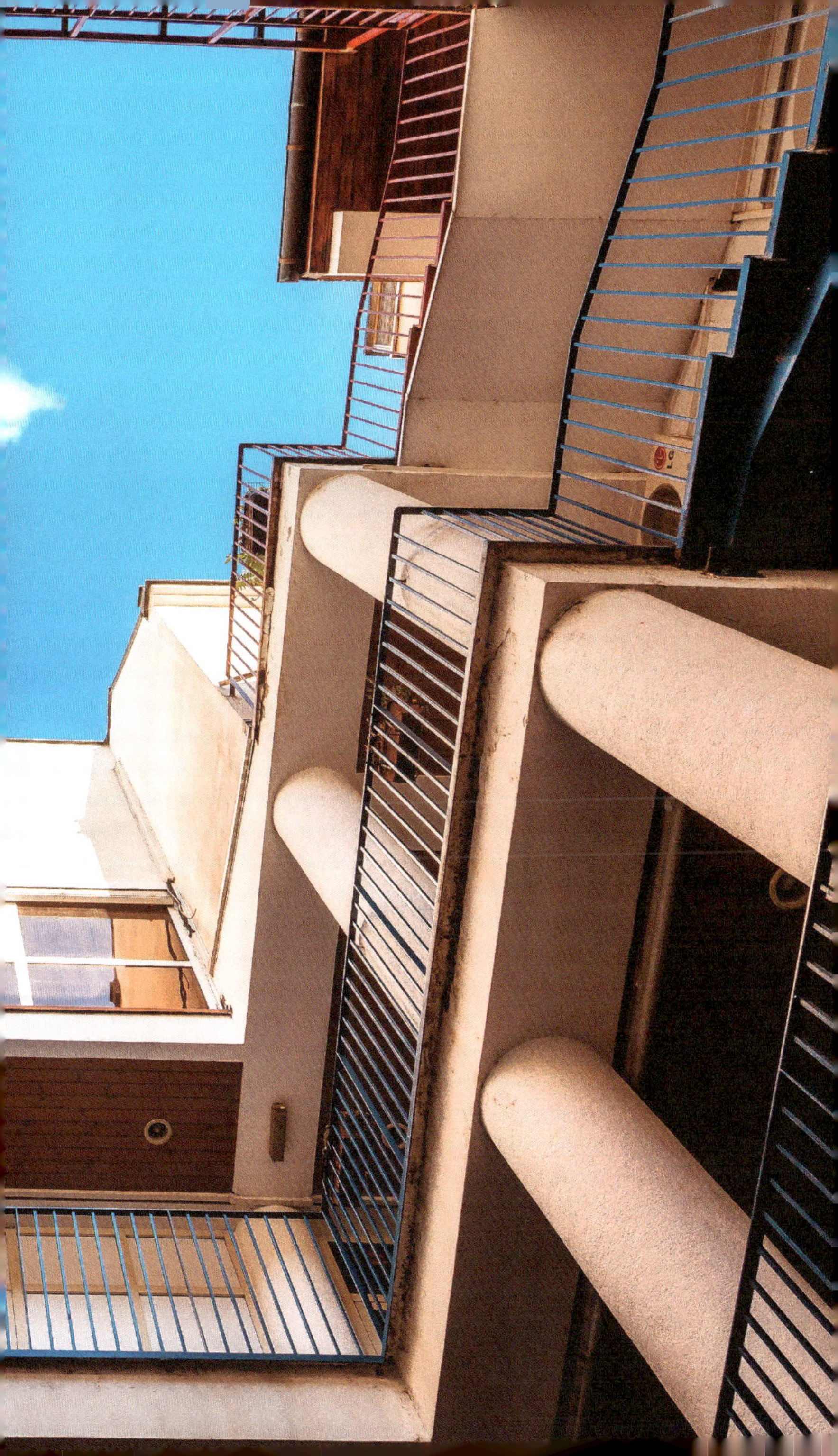

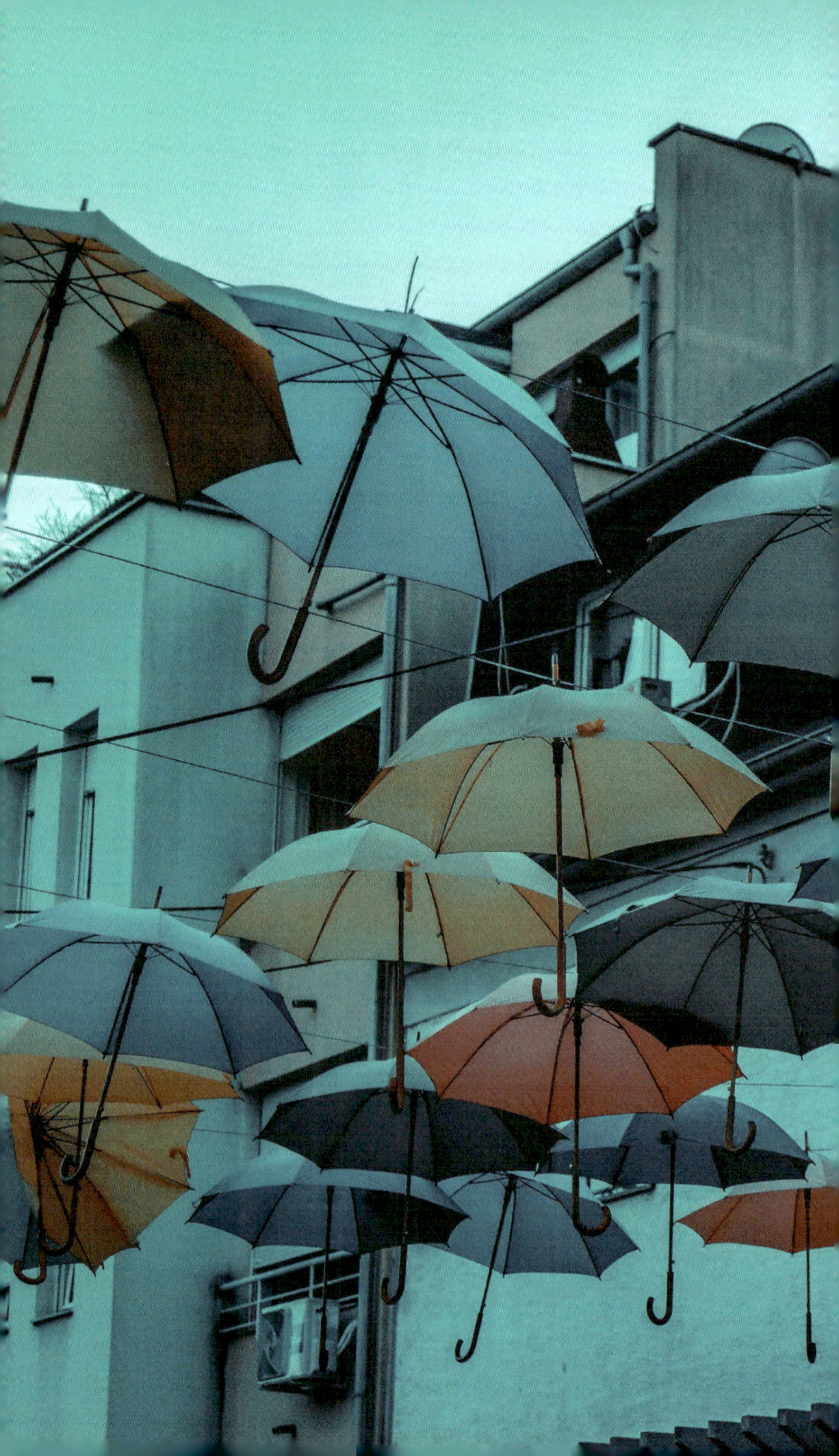

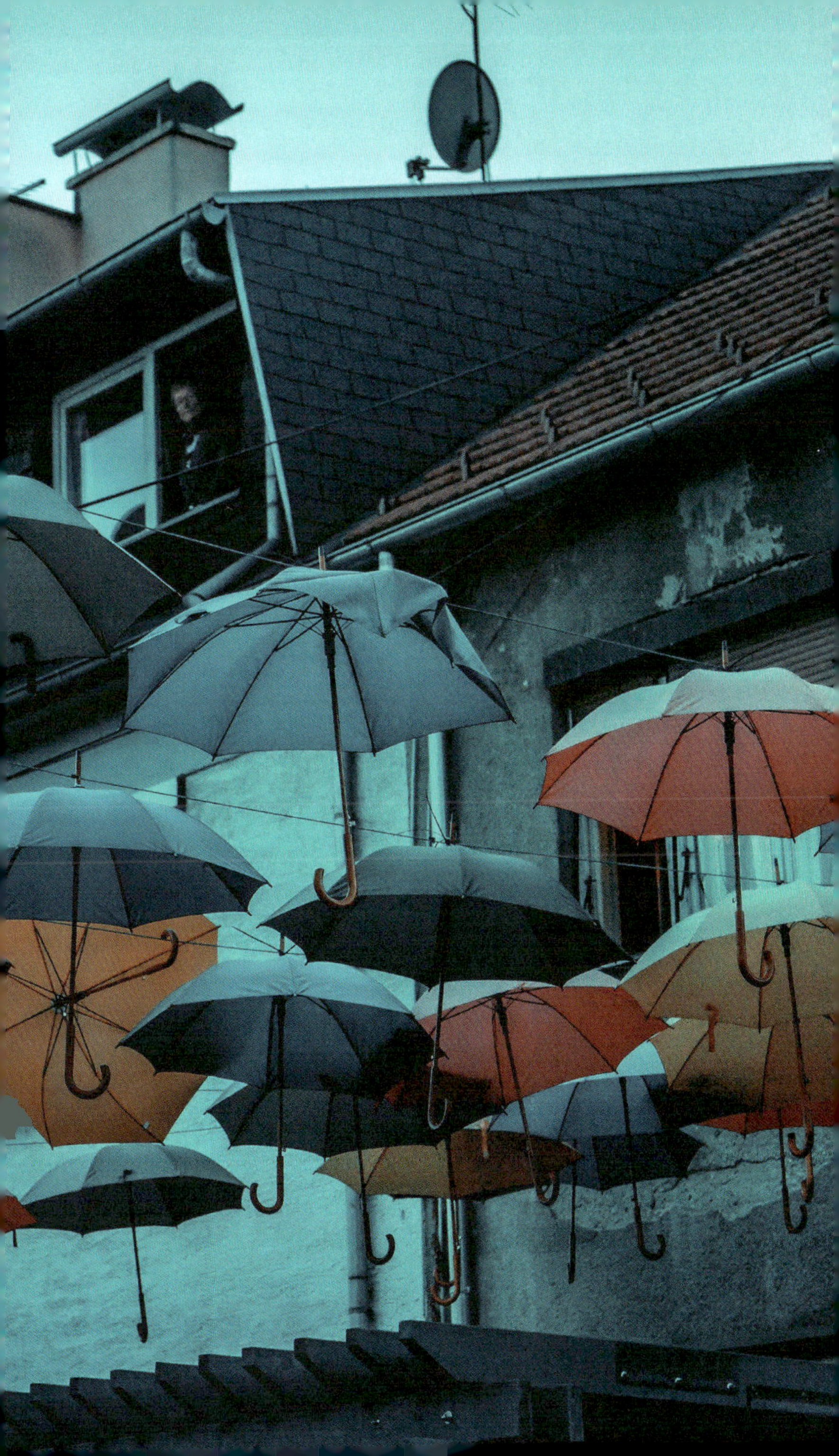

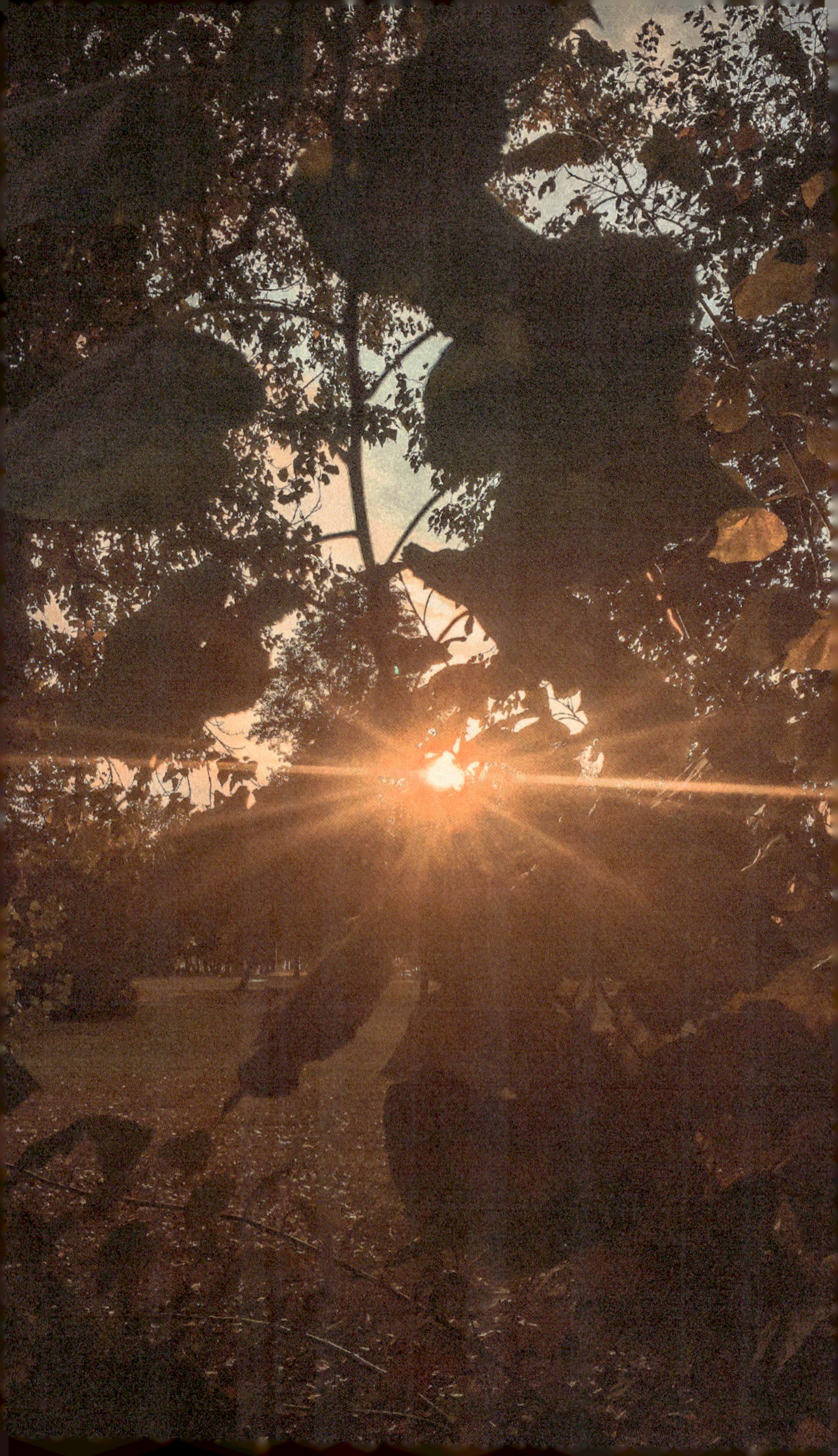

"I think it's part of my personality - I love to travel; I love different cultures and philosophies and perspectives on things."
Martin Henderson

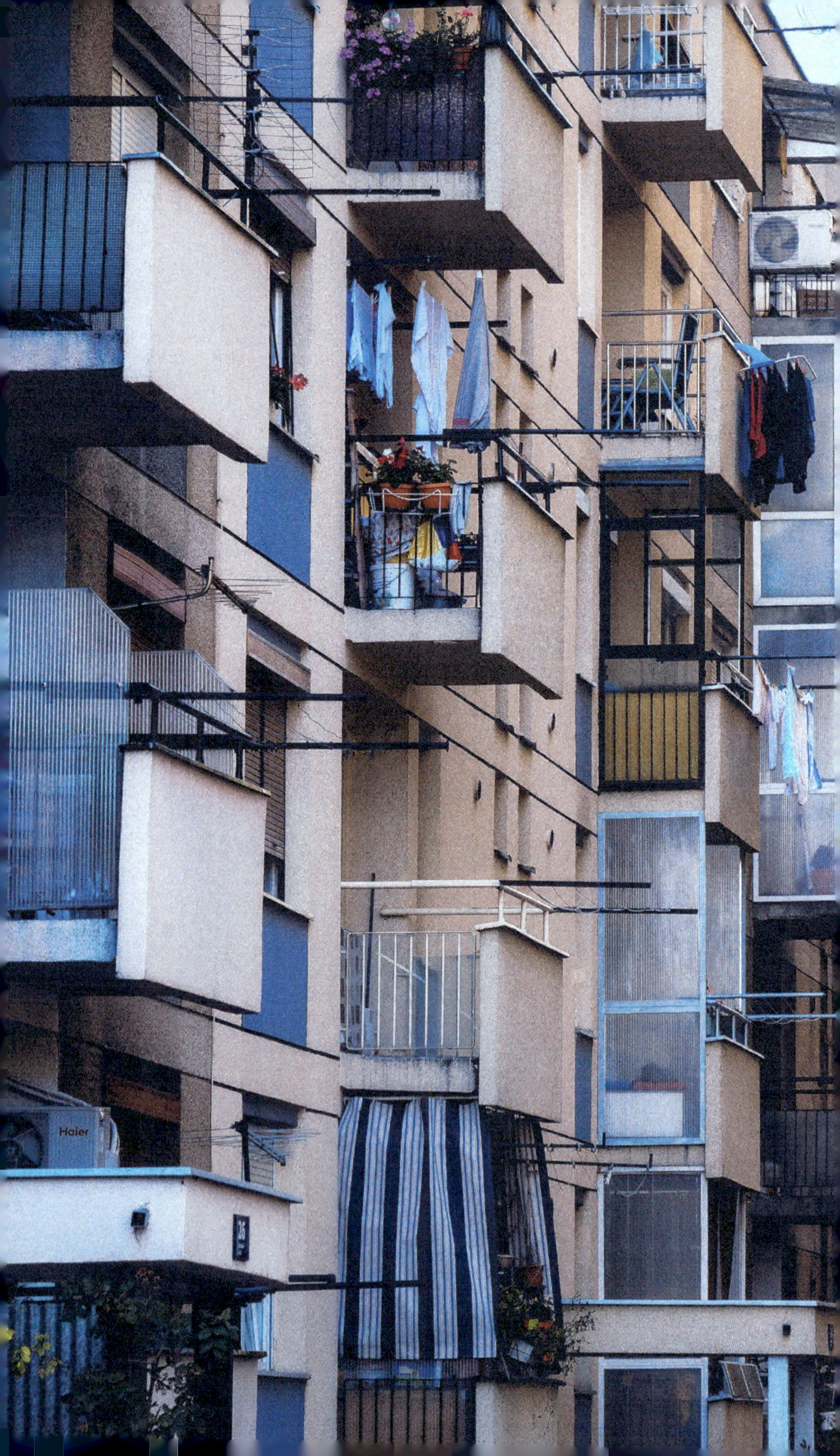
Haier

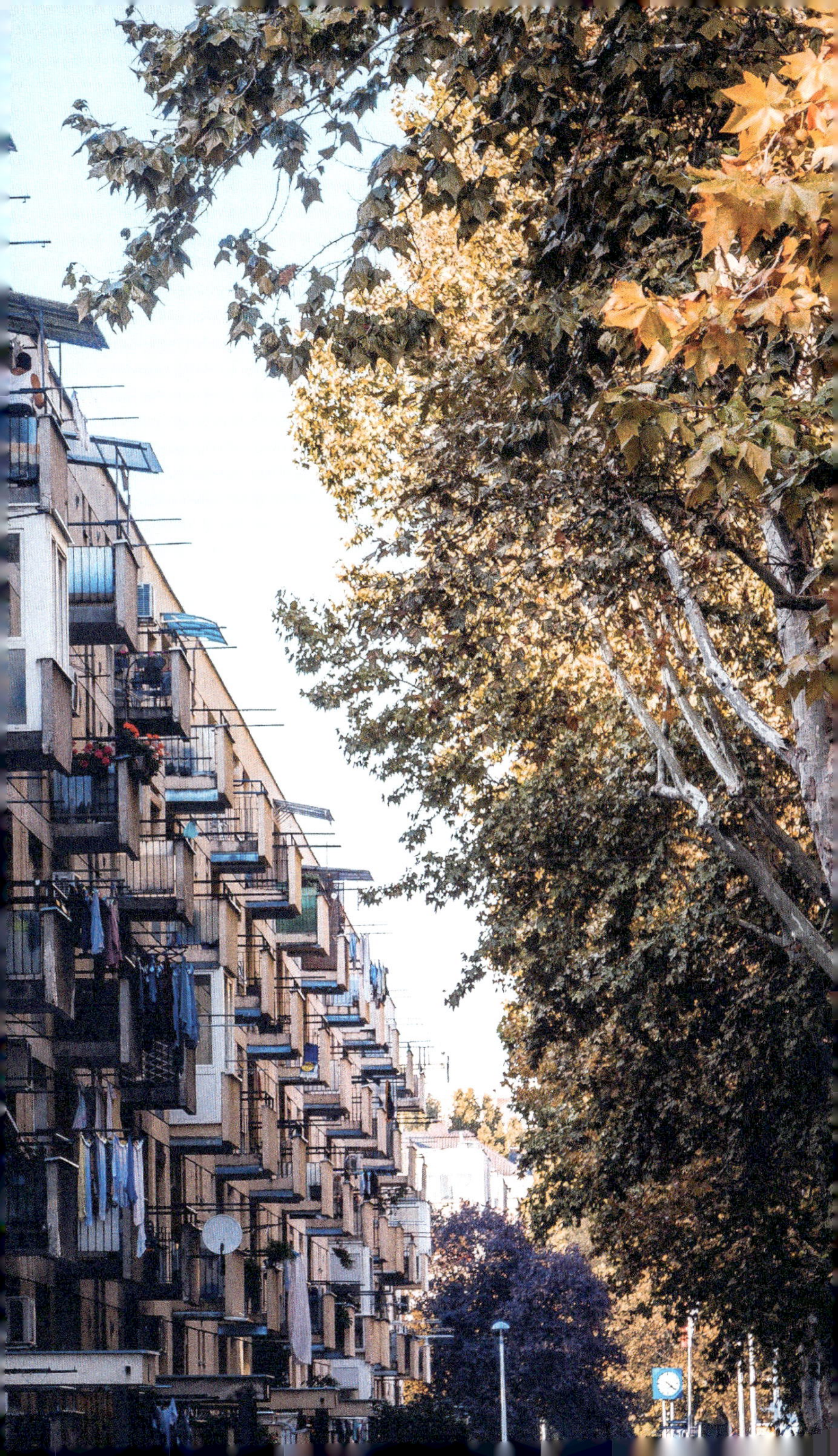

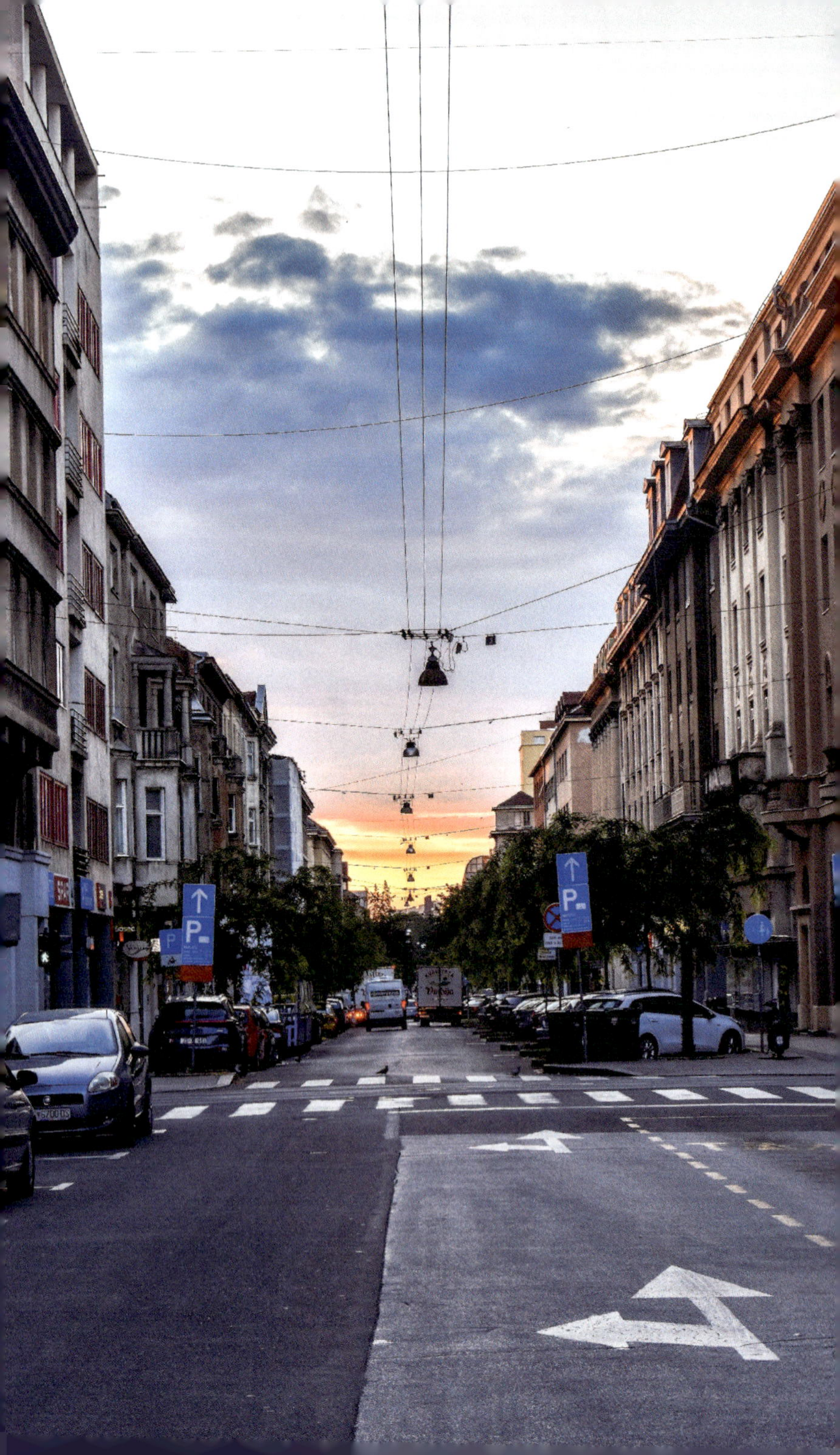
P
P

"If you want to succeed you should strike out on new paths, rather than travel the worn paths of accepted success."
John D. Rockefeller

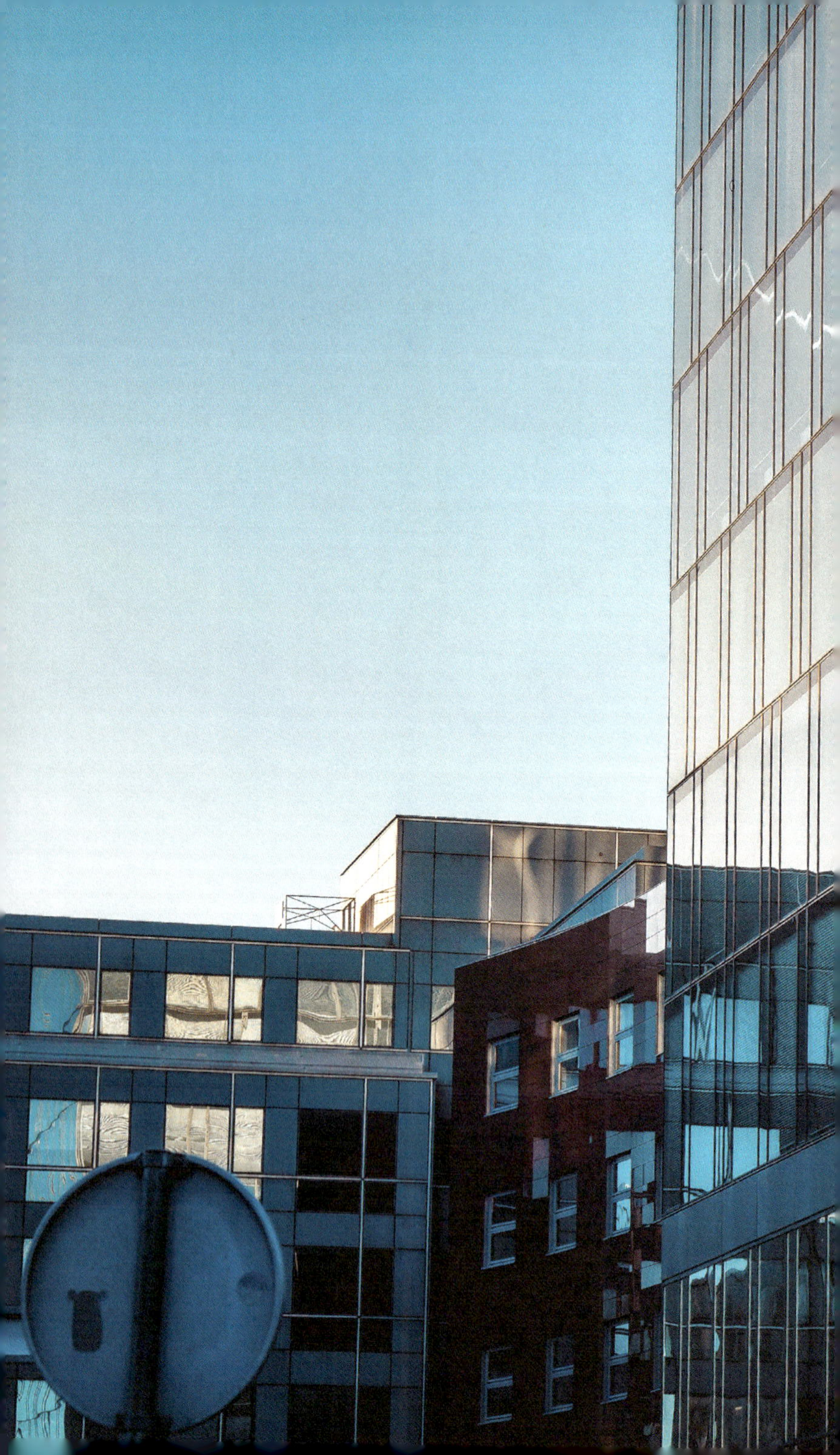

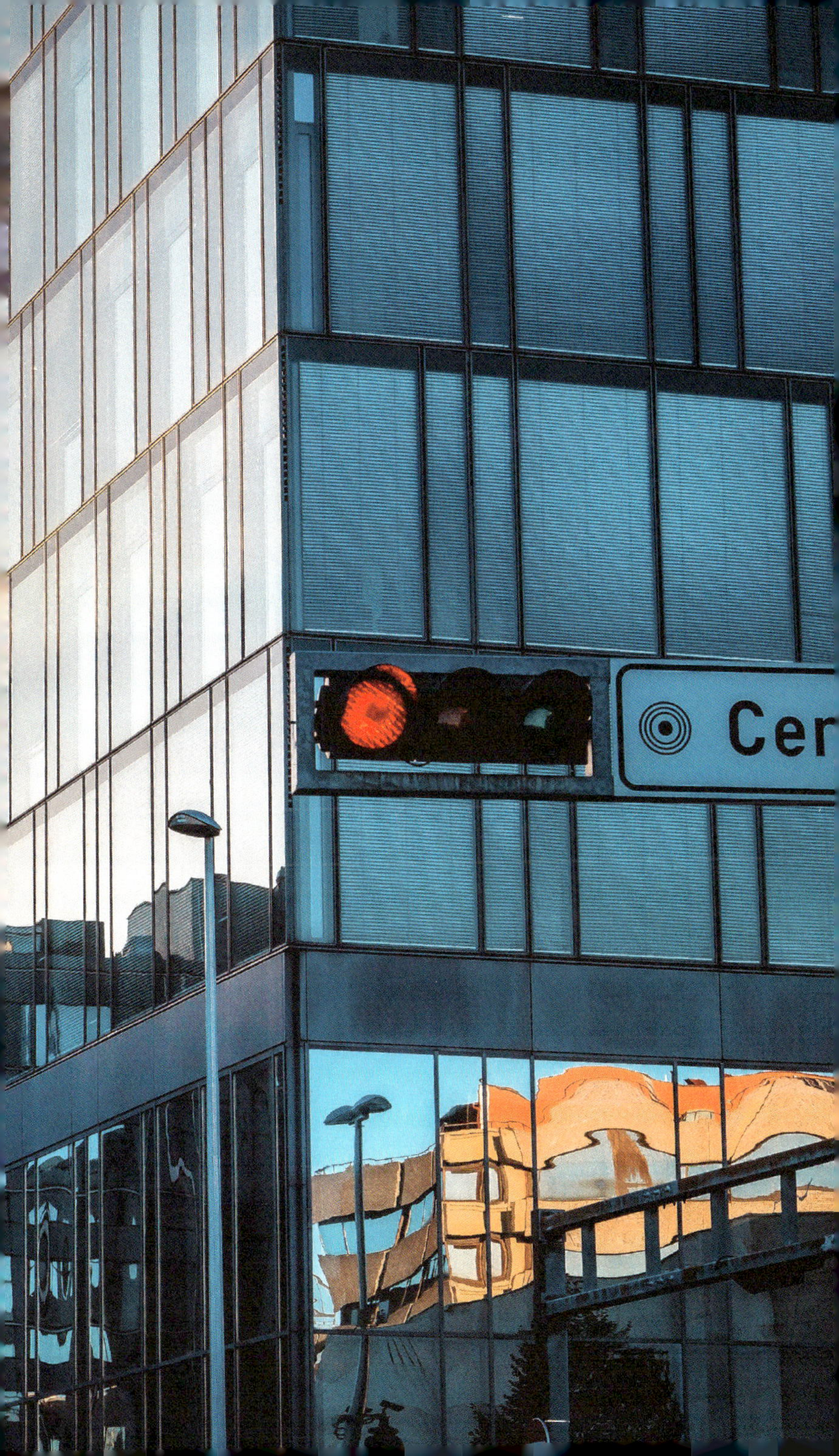
Cer

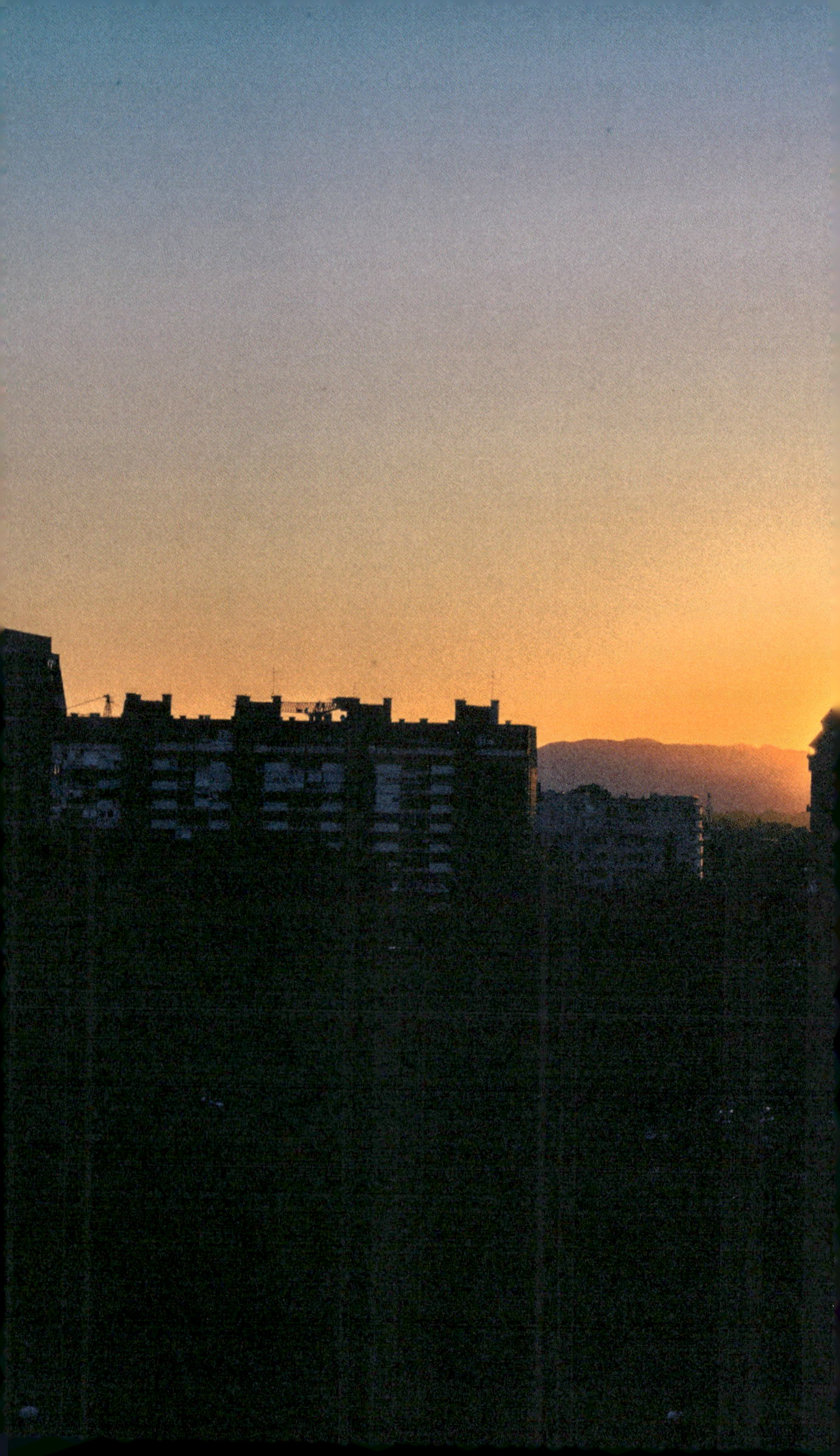

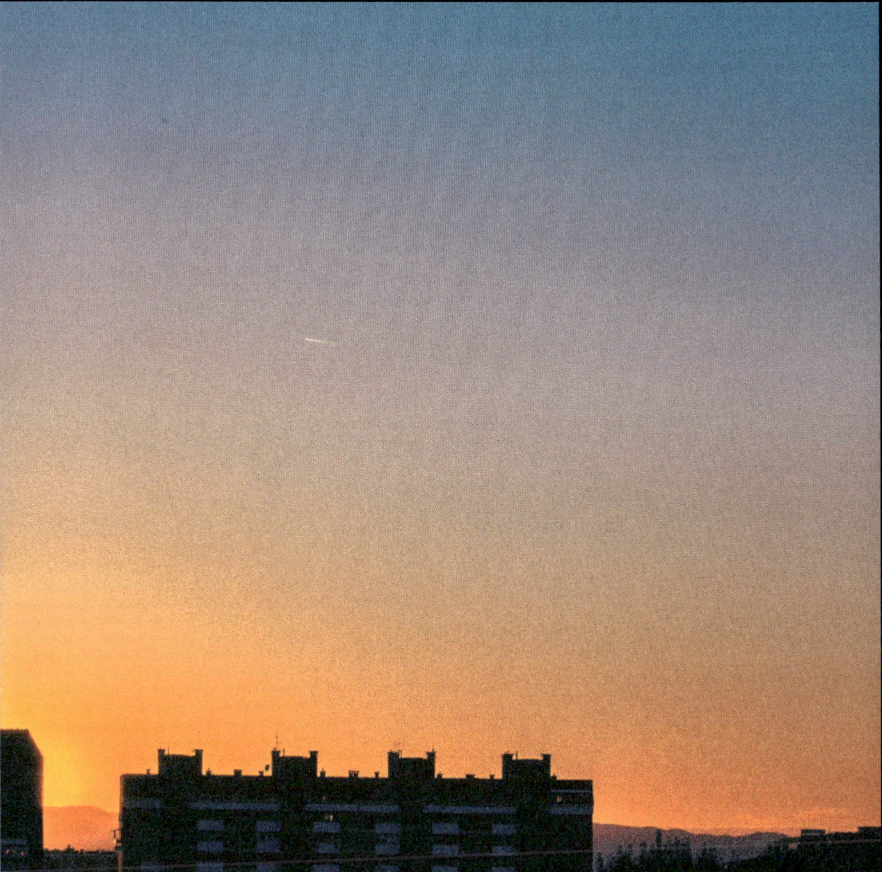

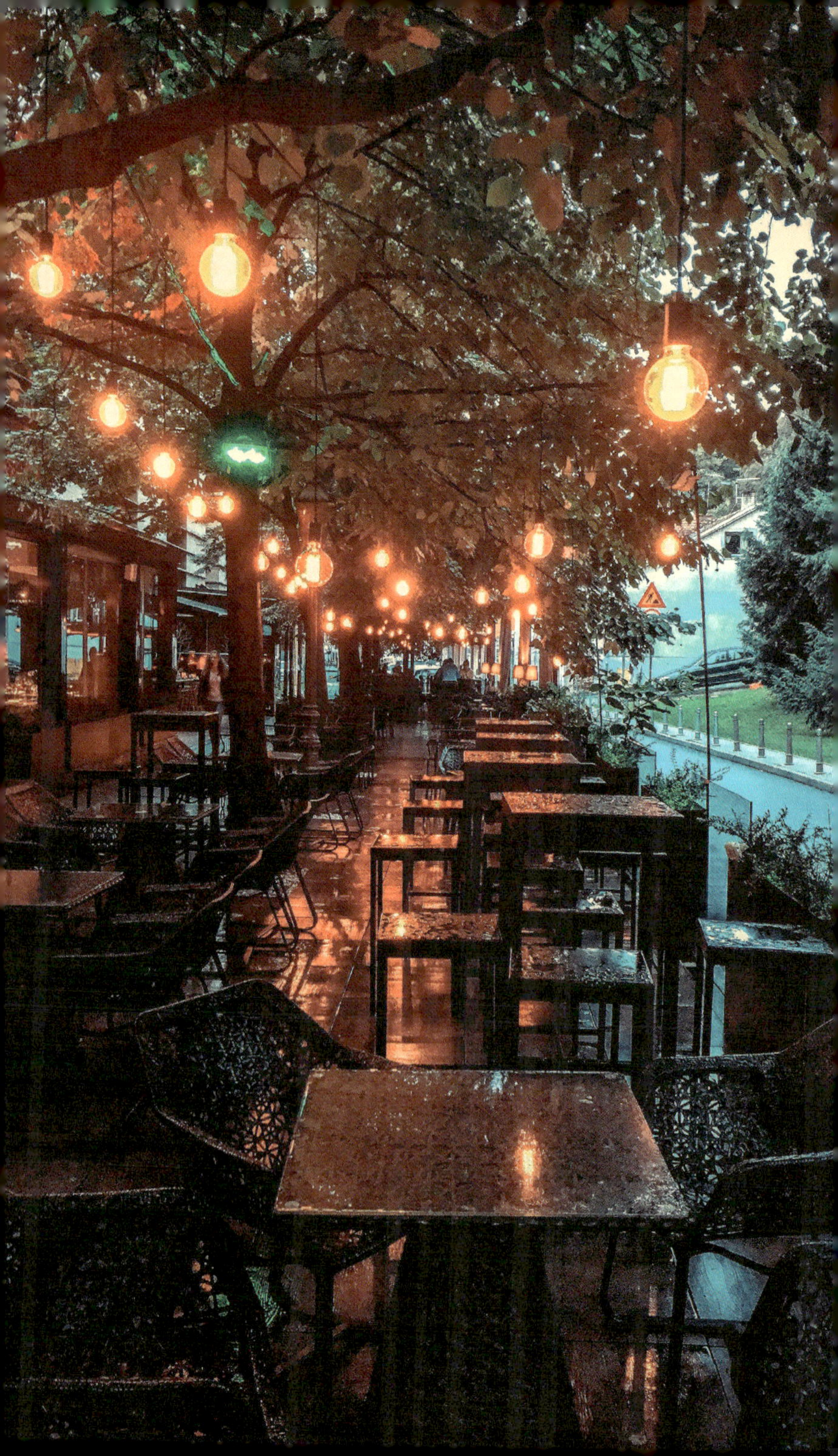

"The person attempting to travel two roads at once will get nowhere."
Xun Kuang

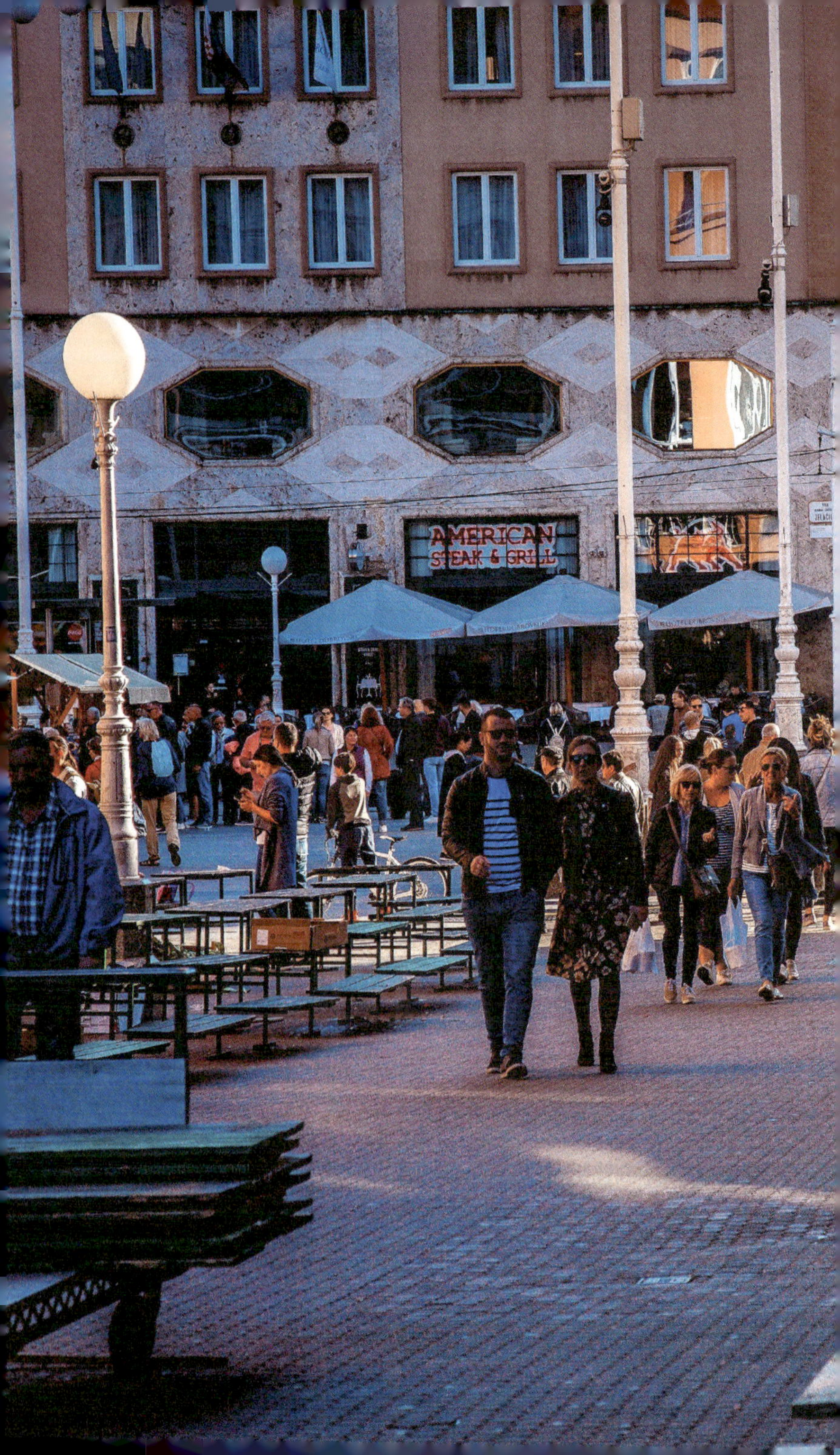
AMERICAN
STEAK & GRILL

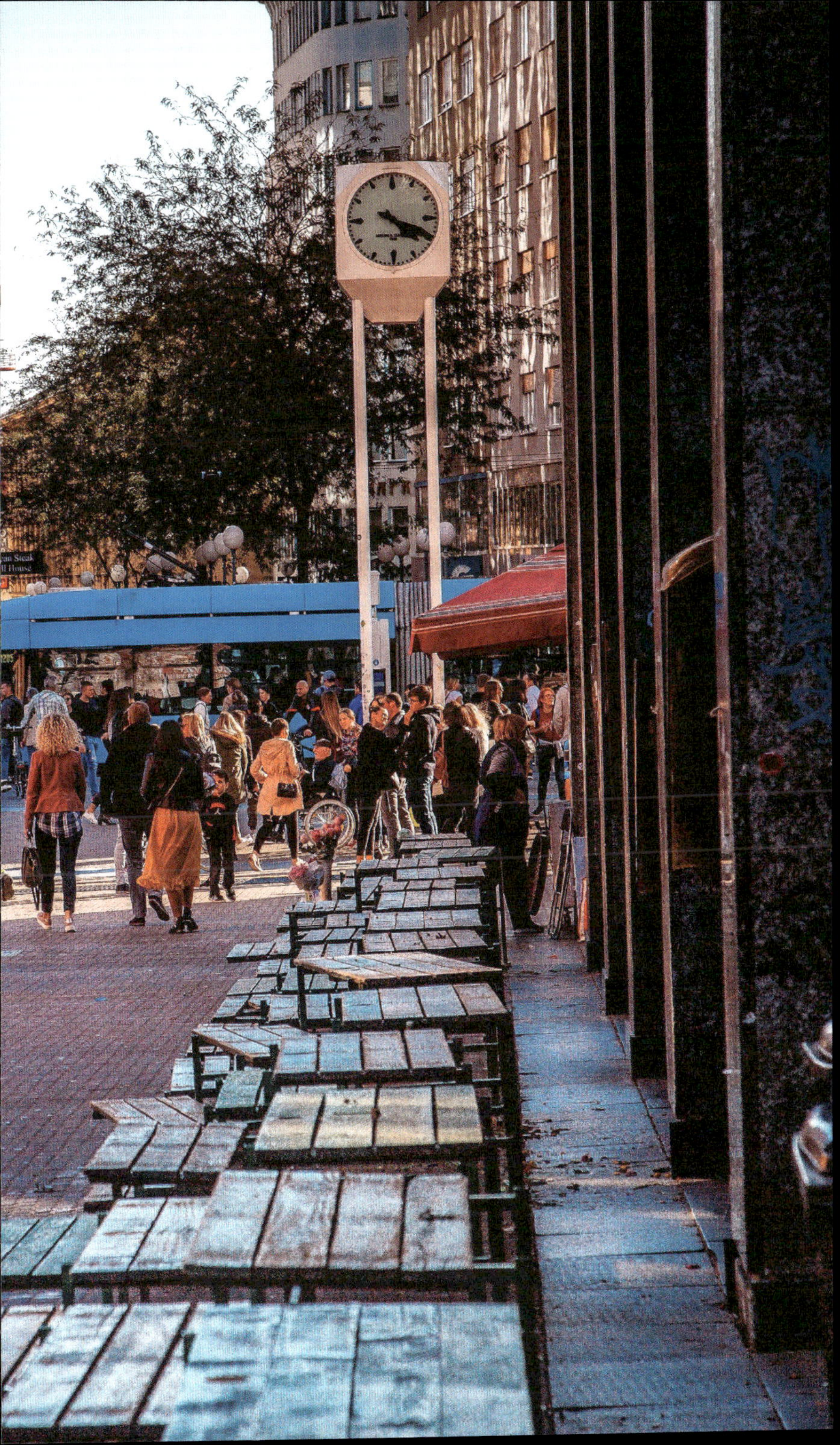

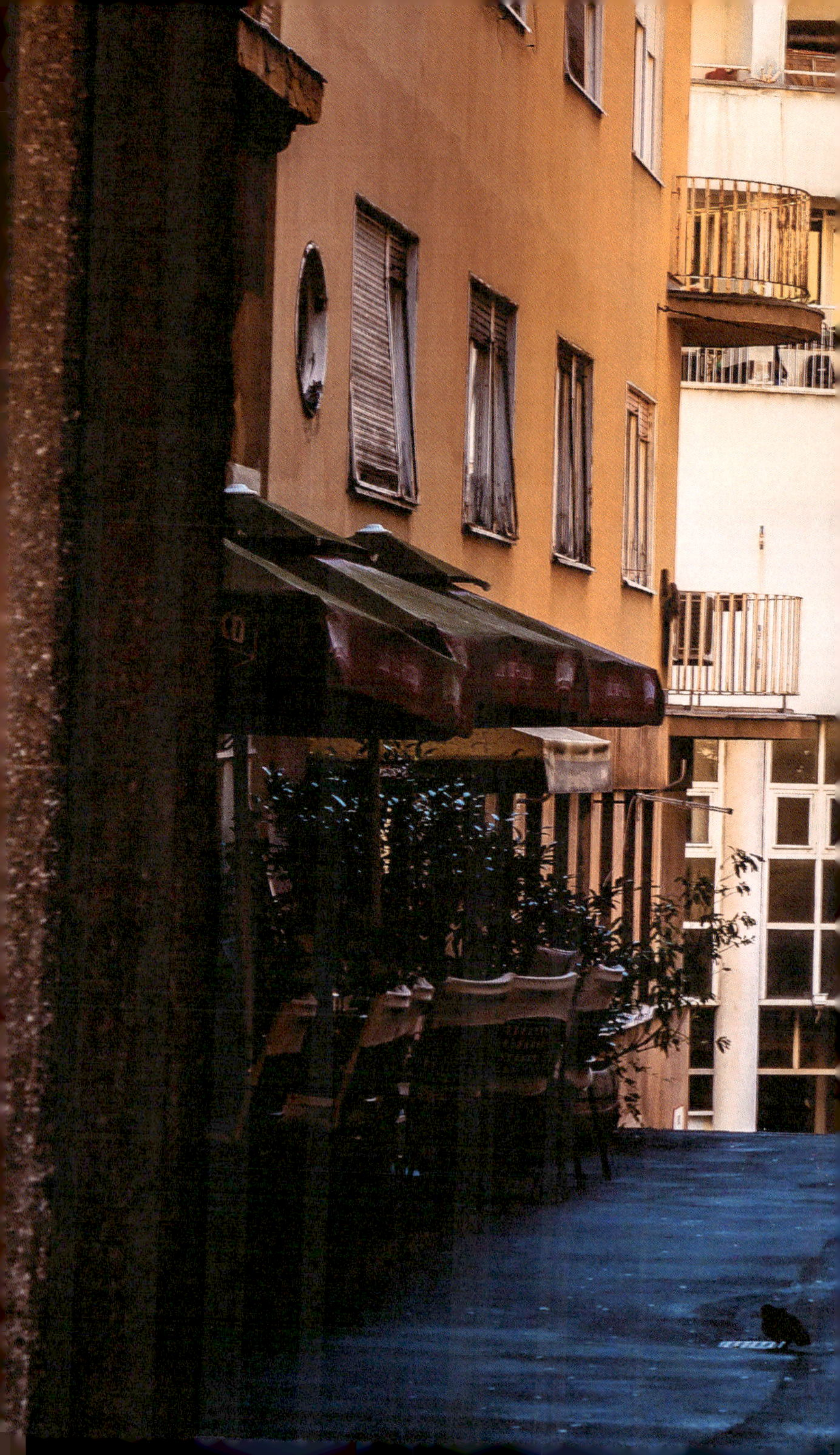

SAPHIR

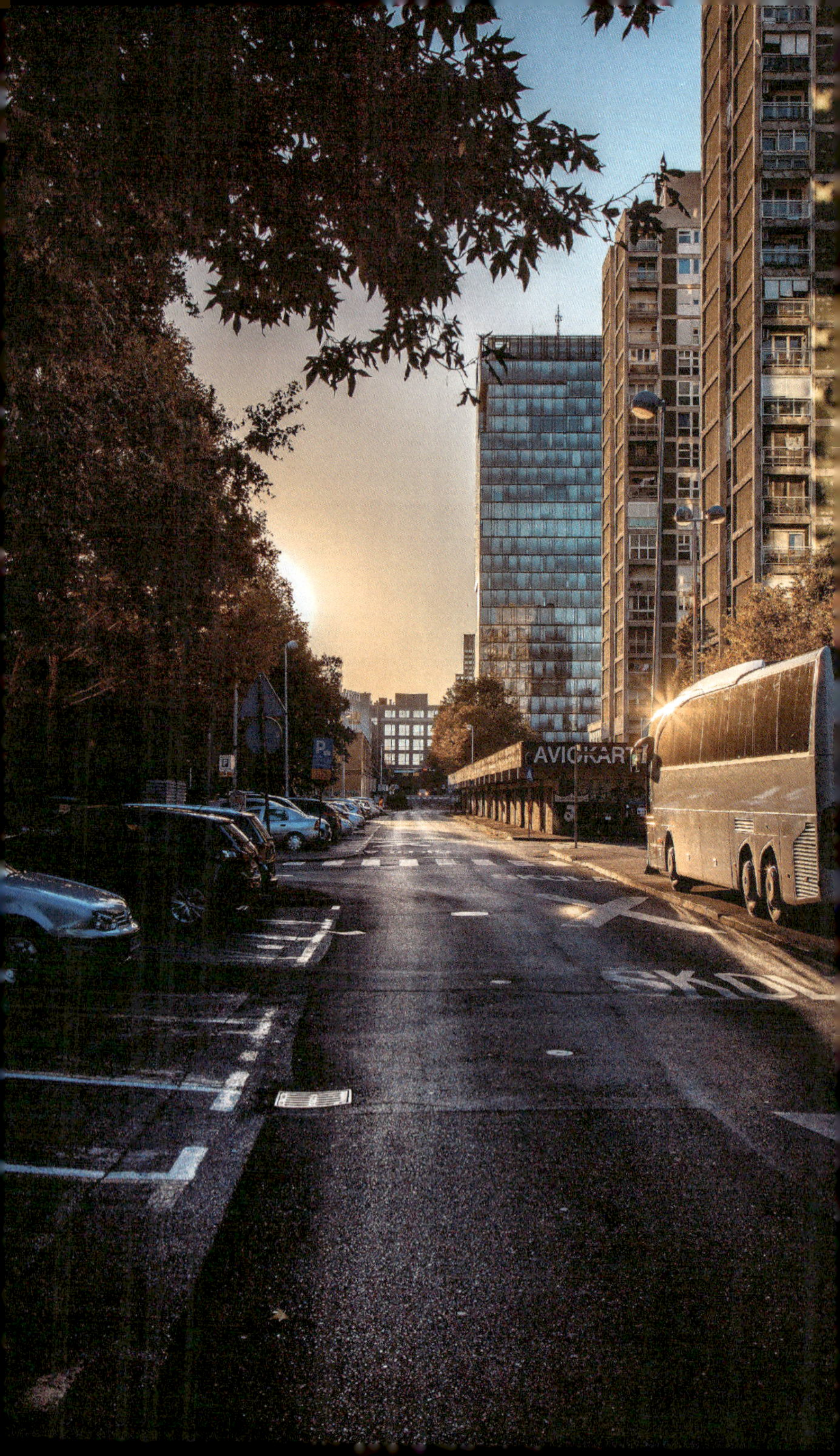
AVIOKART

"We are making photographs to understand what our lives mean to us."
Ralph Hattersley

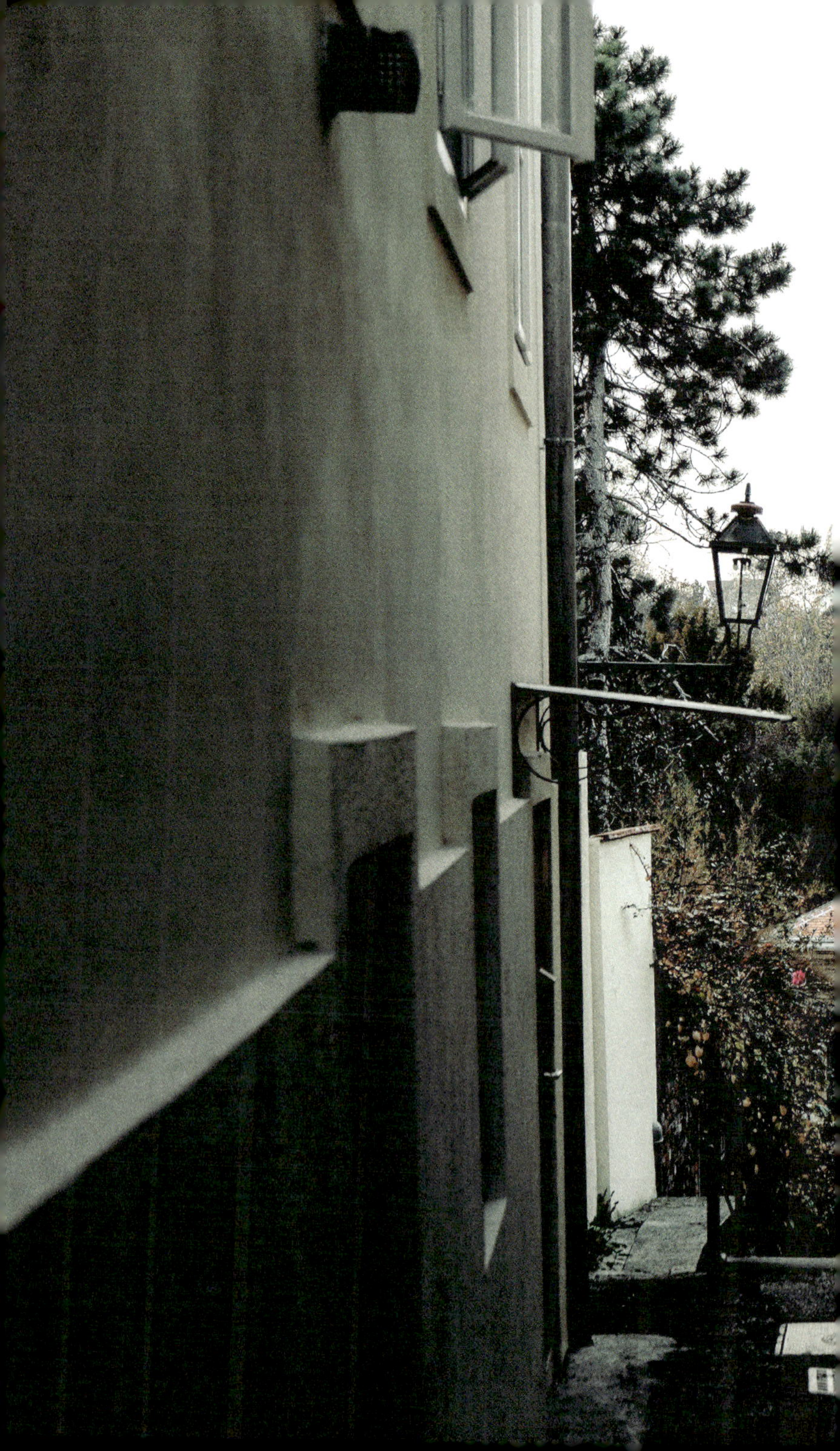

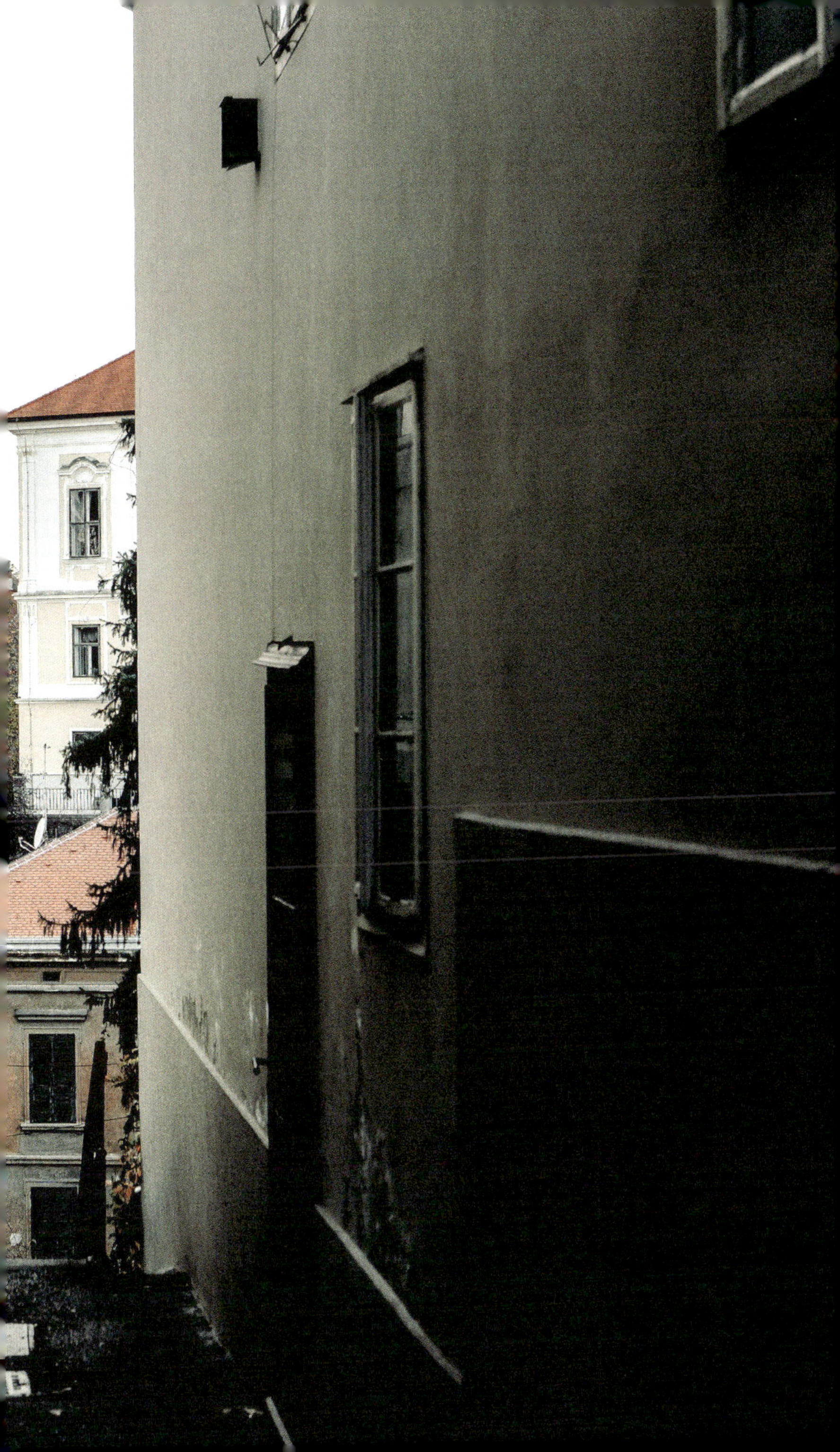

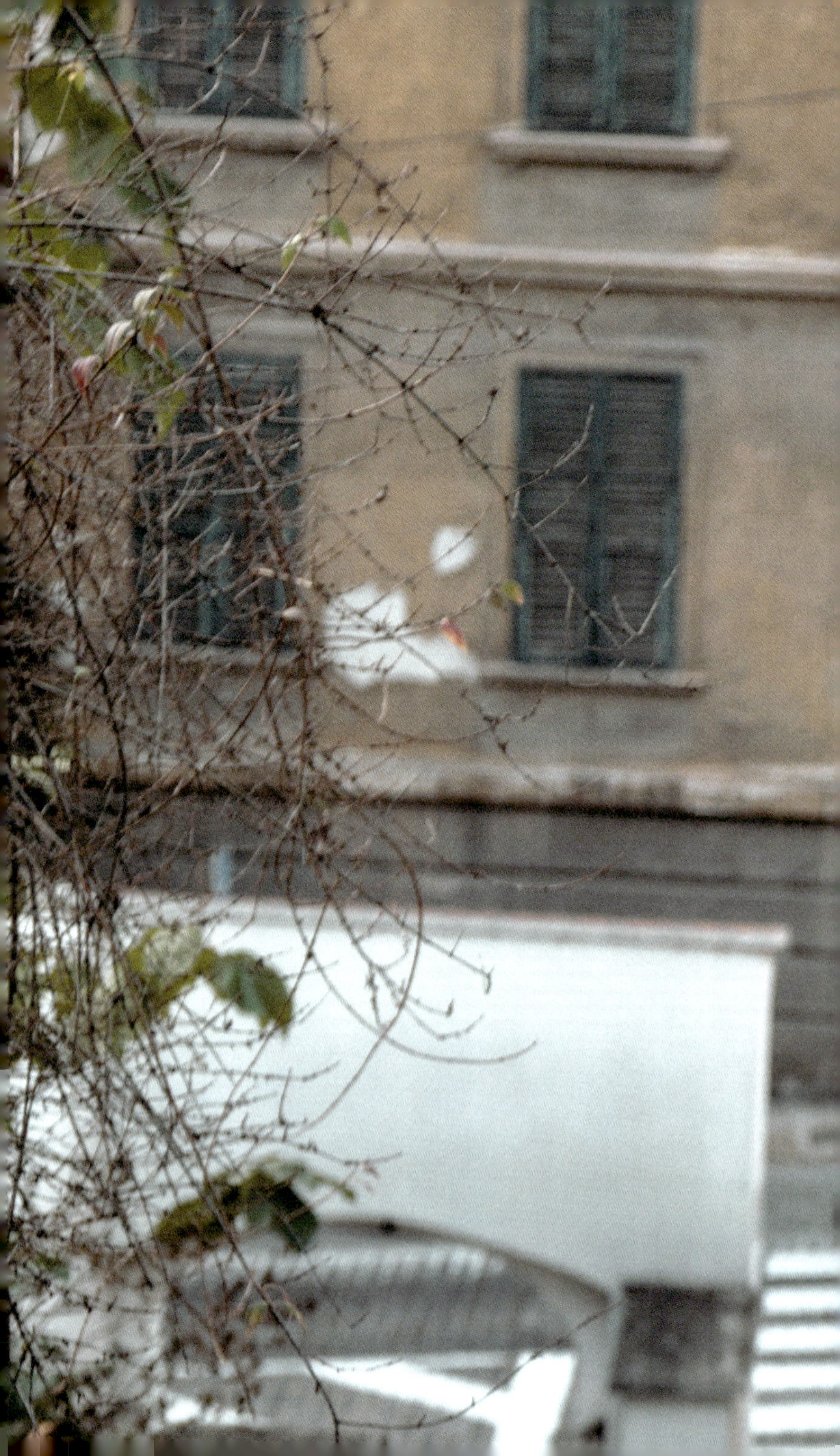

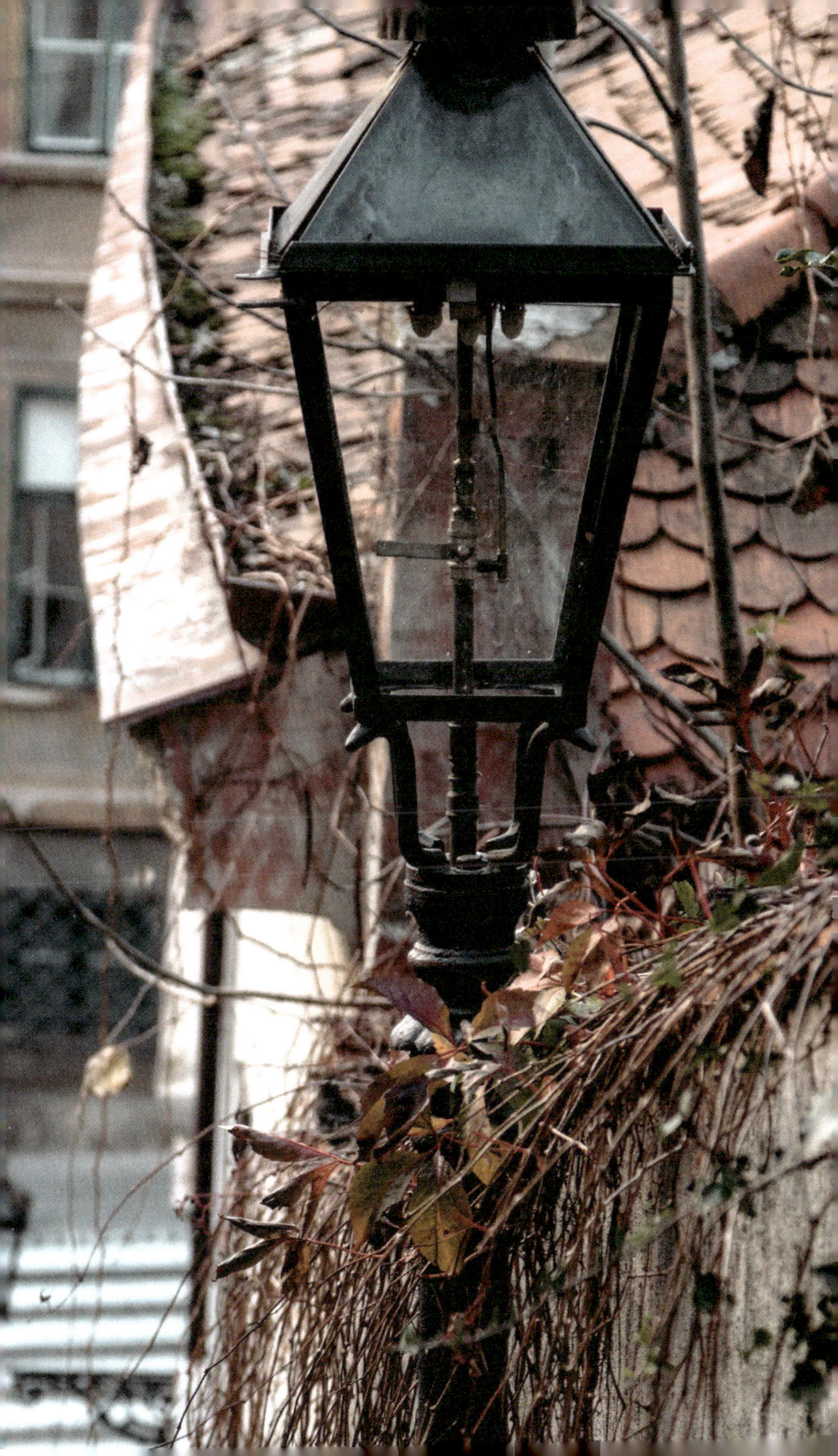

"You don't take a photograph. You ask quietly to borrow it."
Unknown

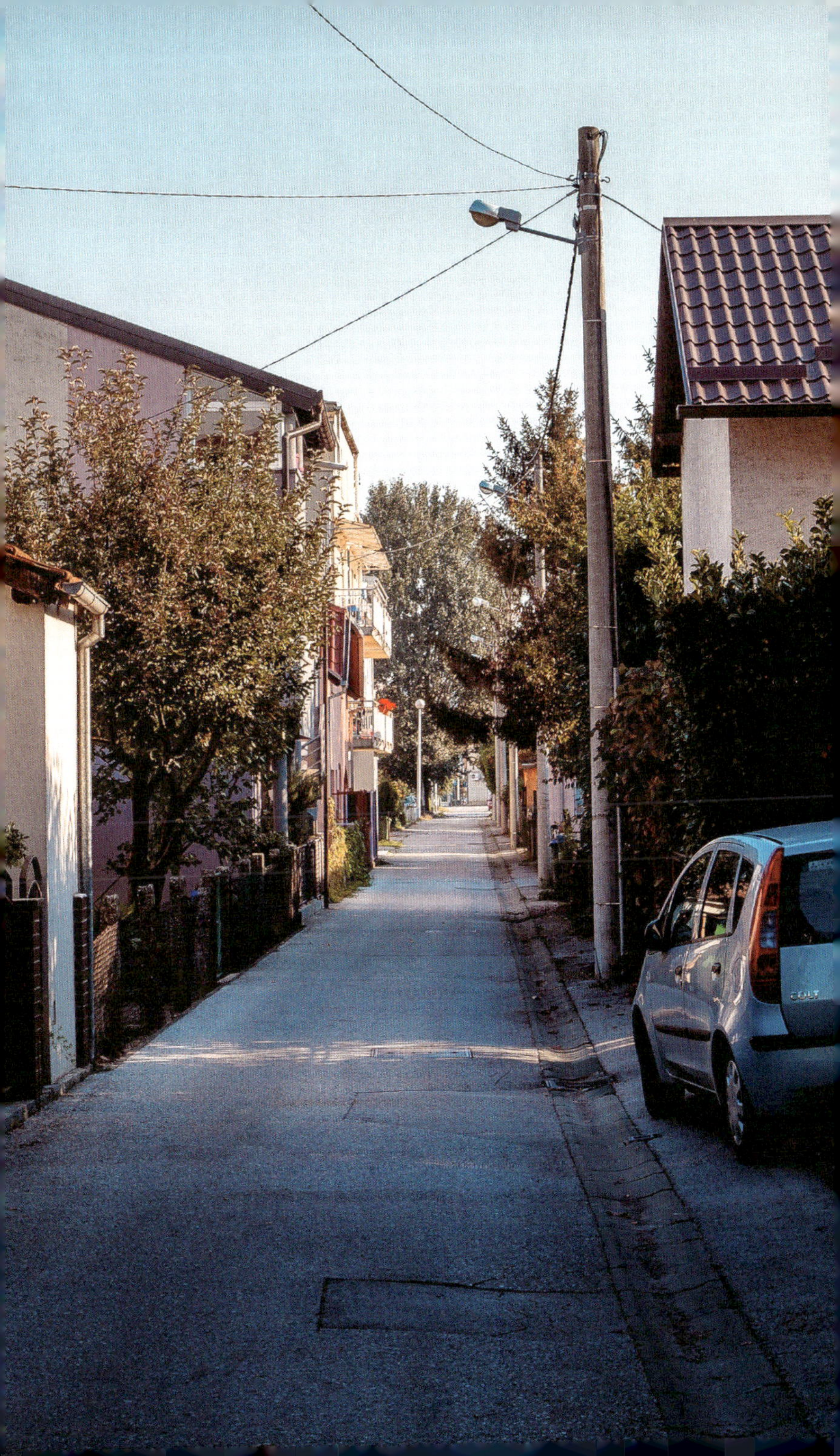

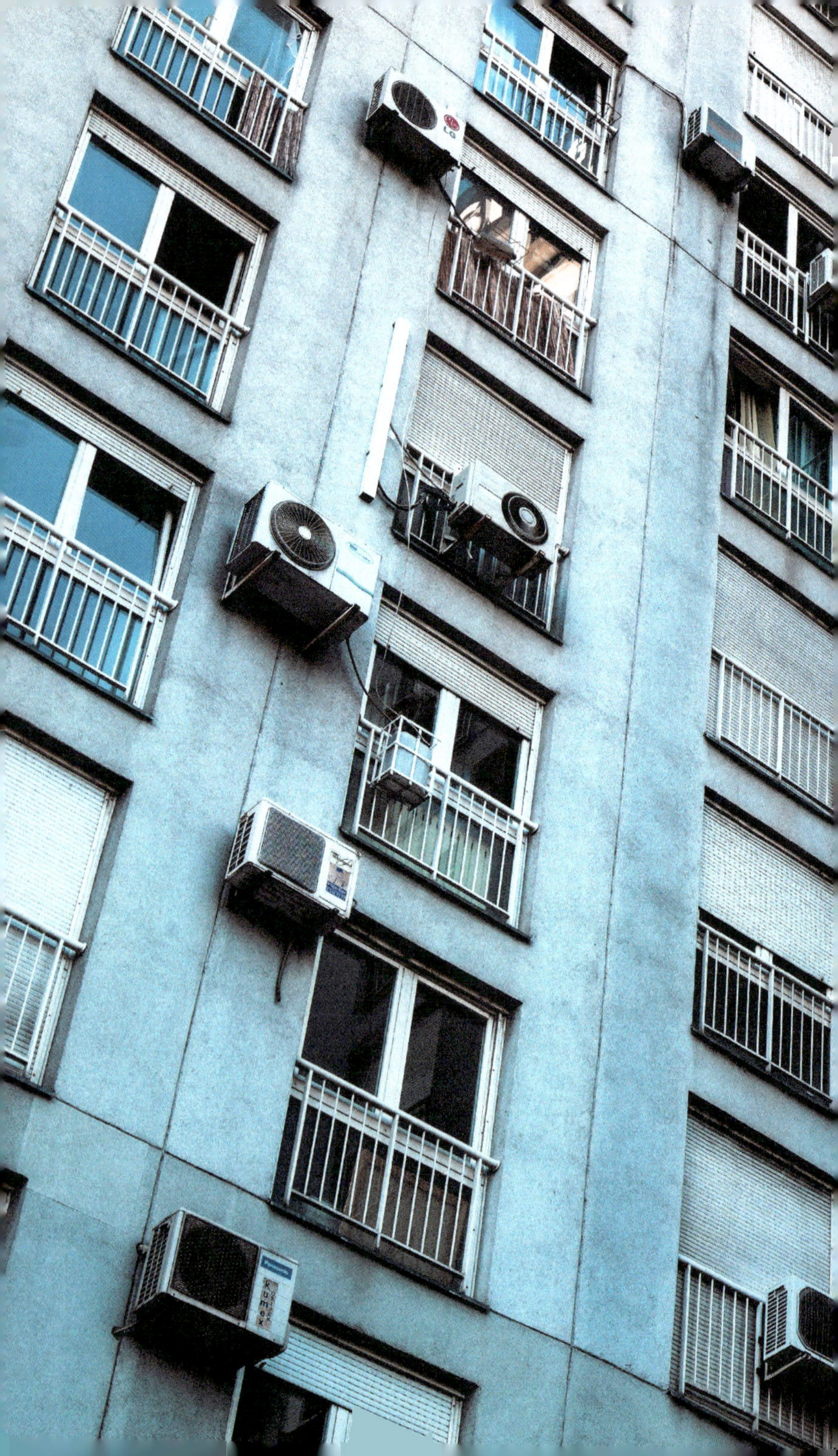

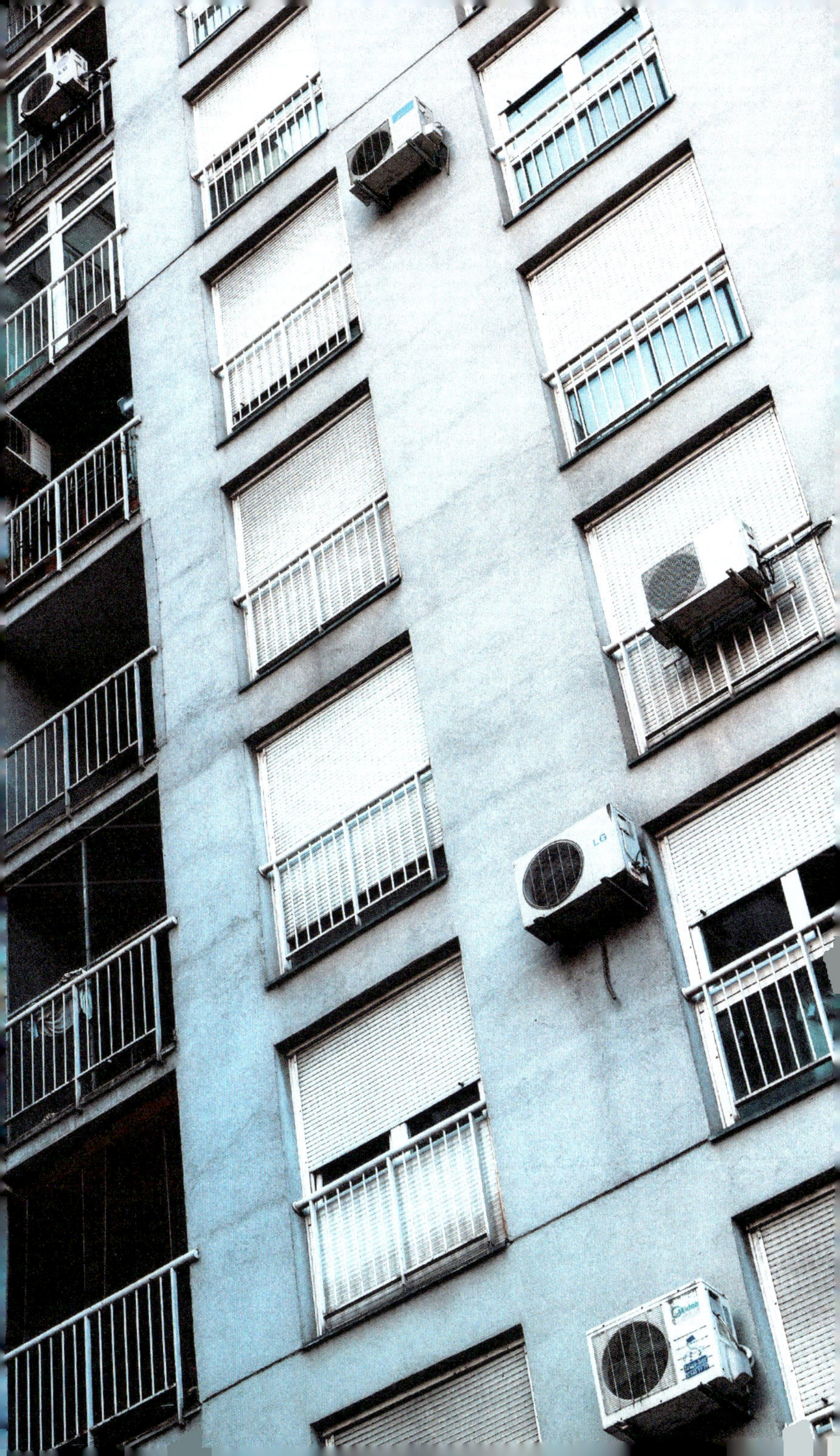
LG

RESTORAN
Mr. Chen

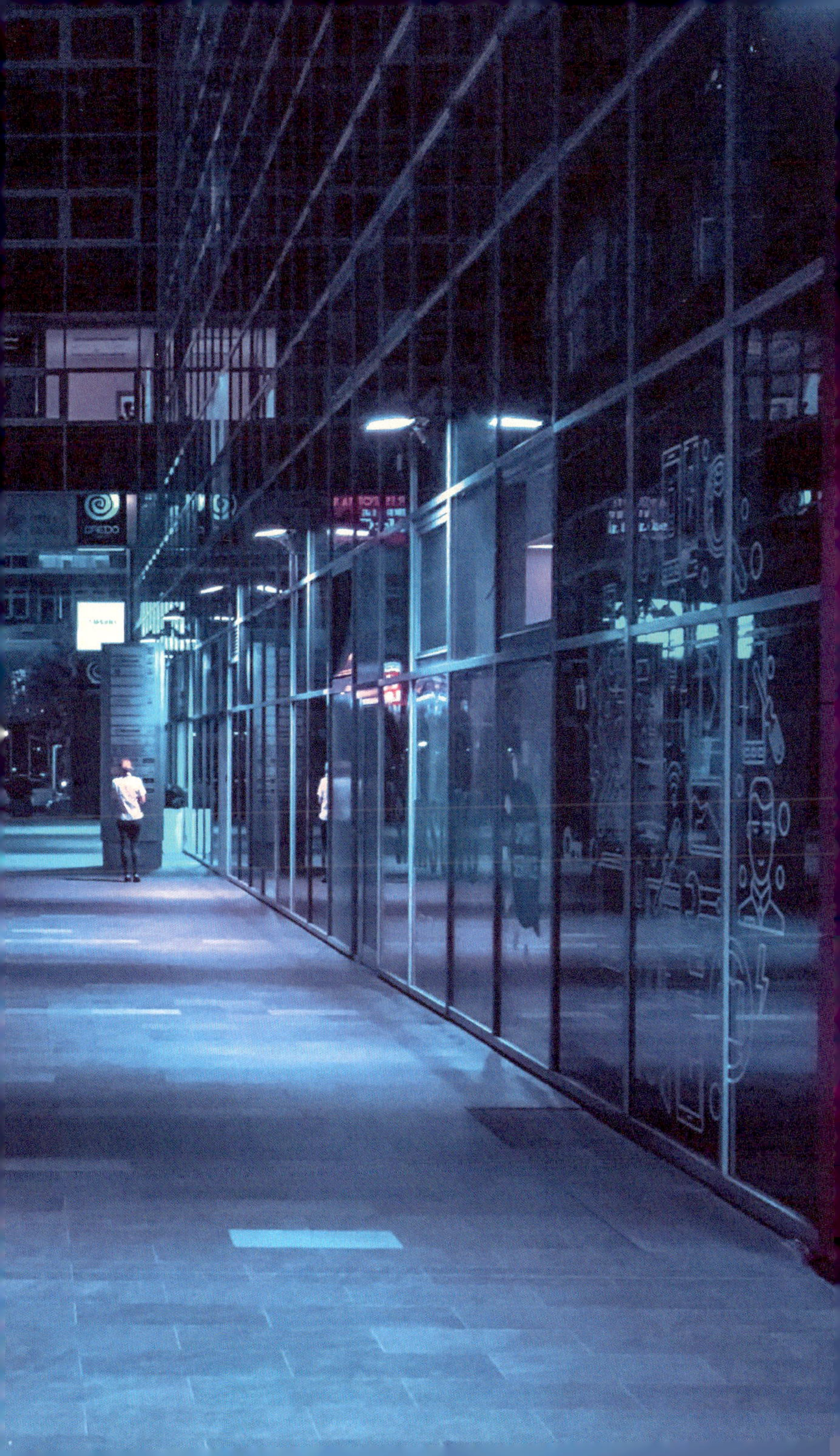

"We are all travelers in the wilderness of this world, and the best we can find in our travels is an honest friend."
Robert Louis Stevenson

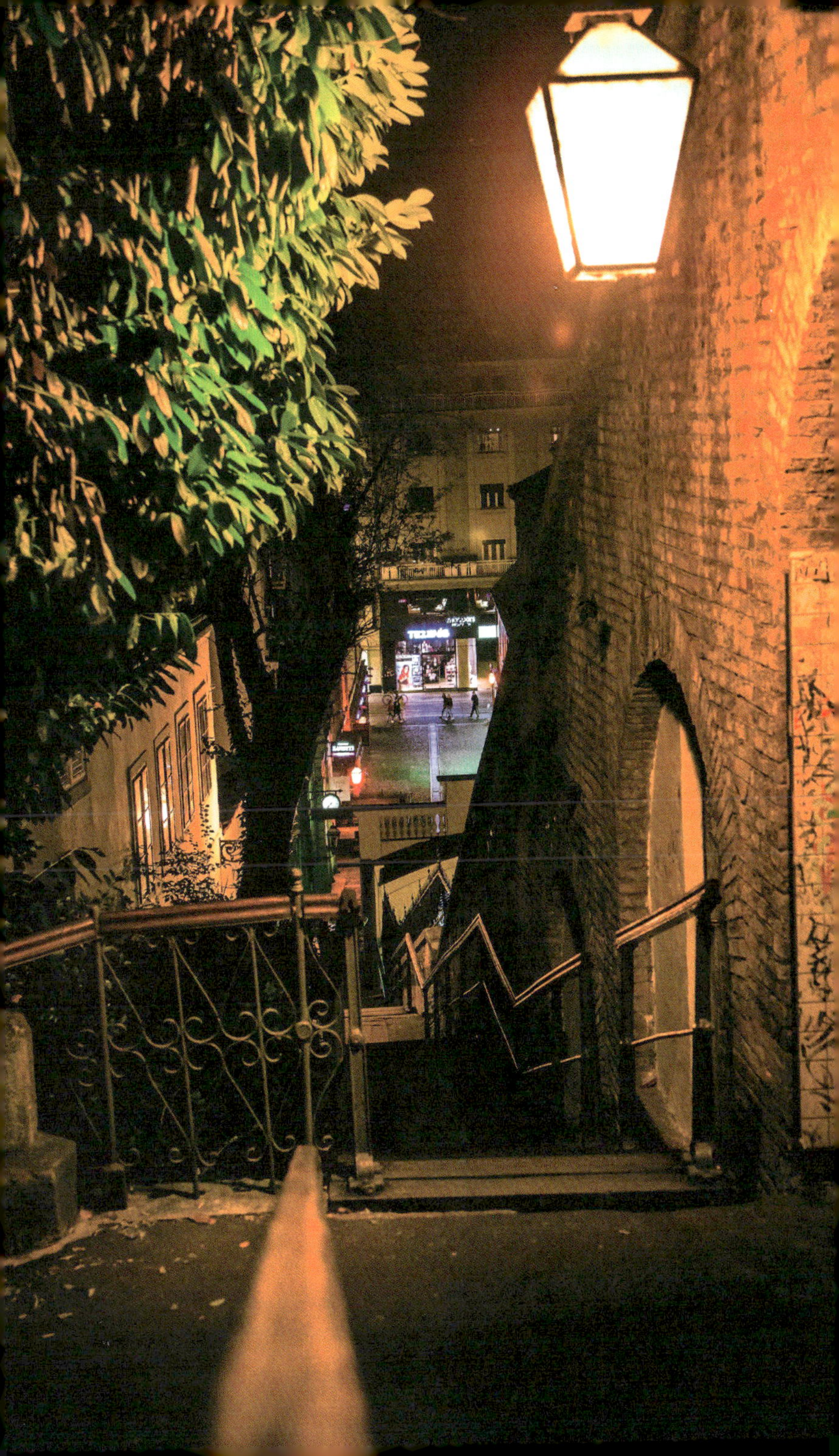

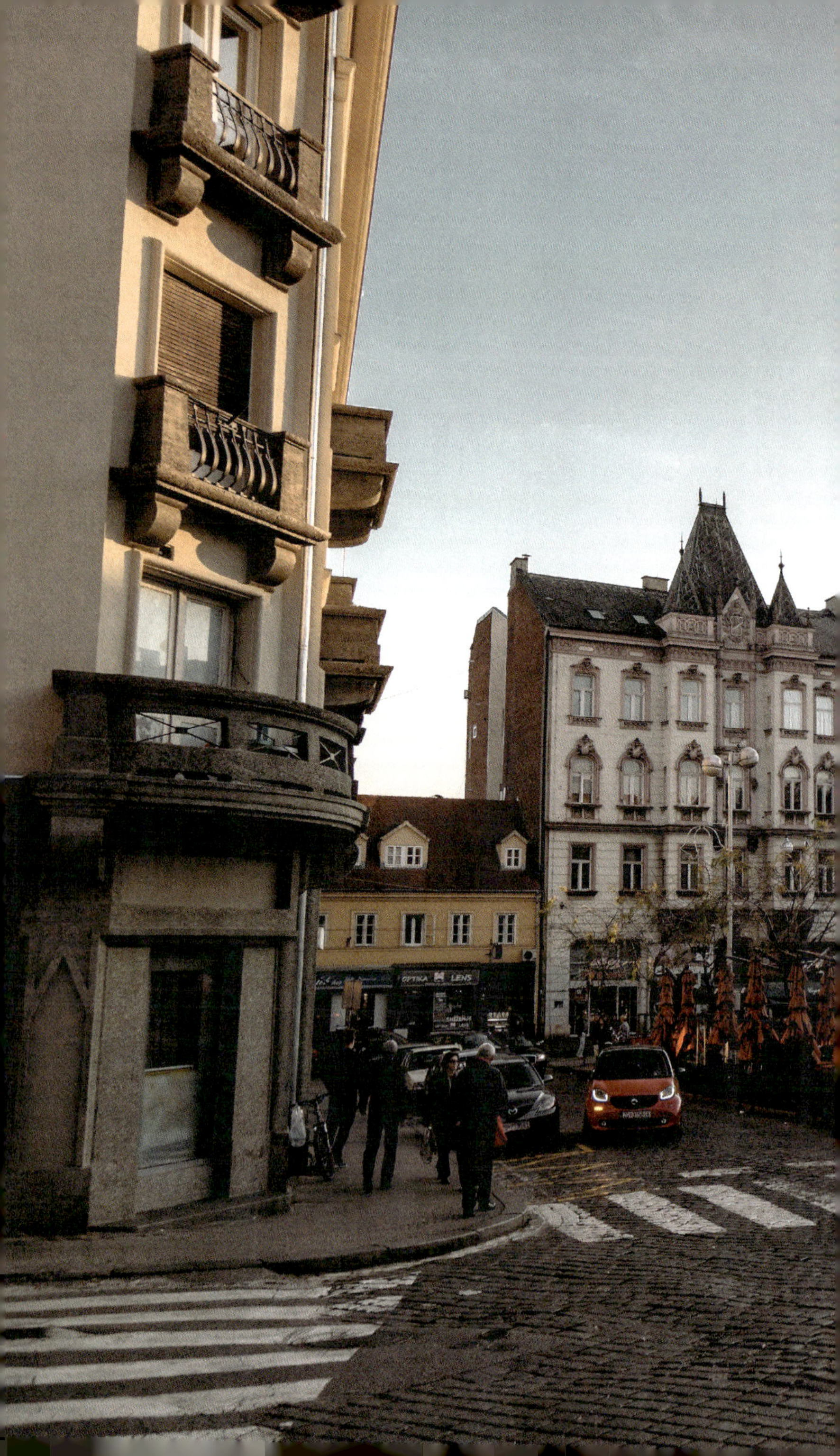
OPTIKA
LENS

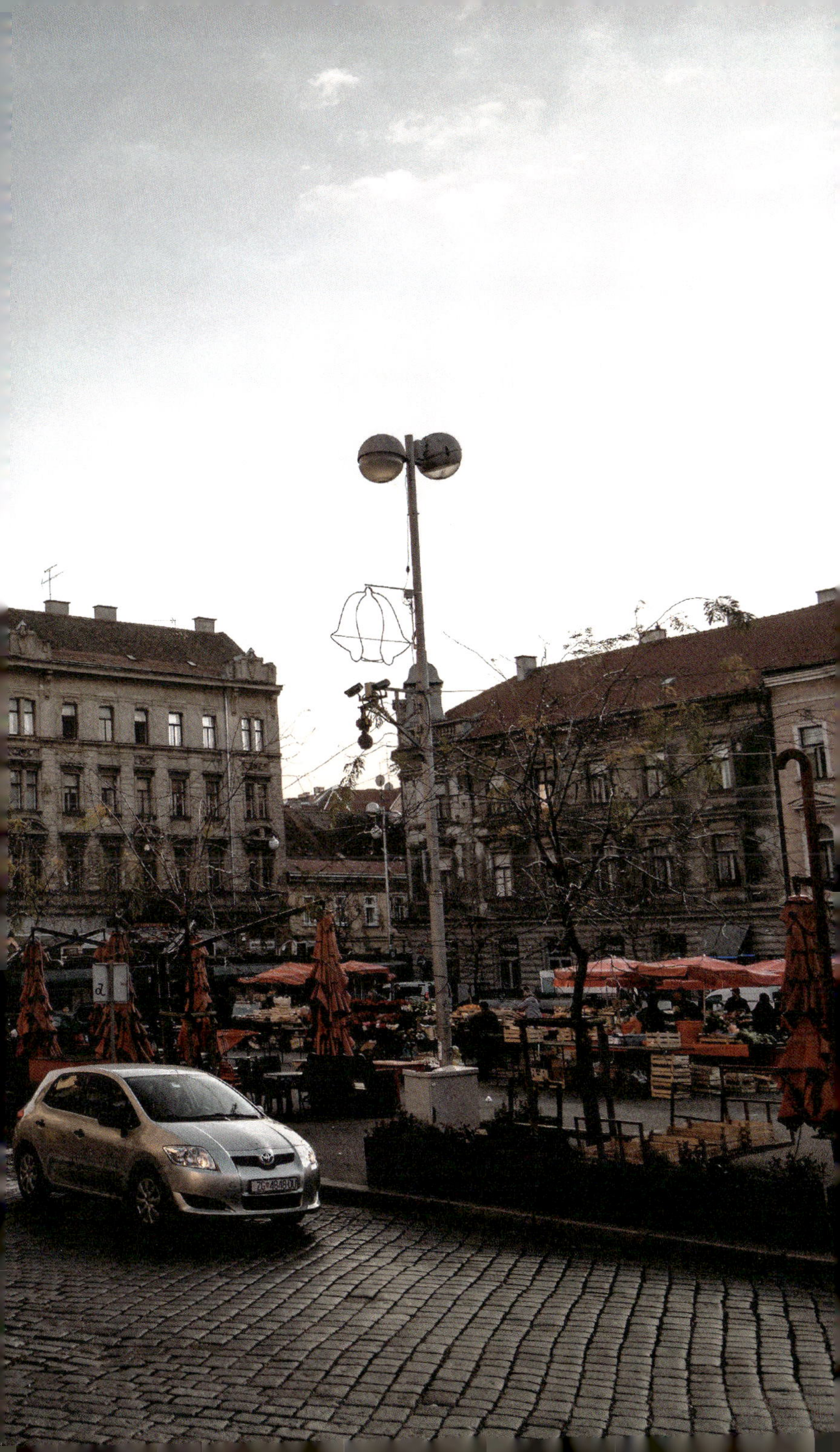

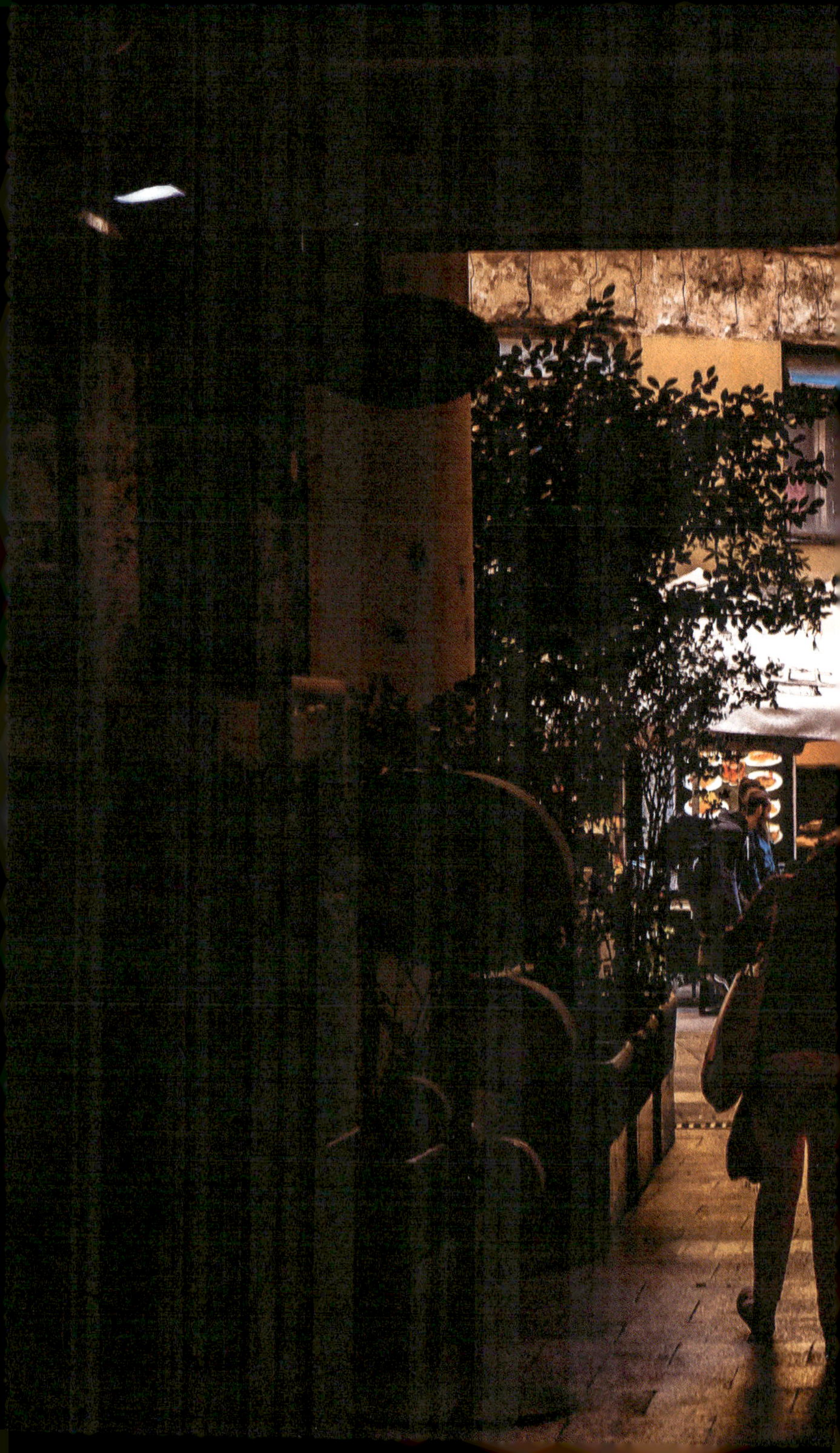

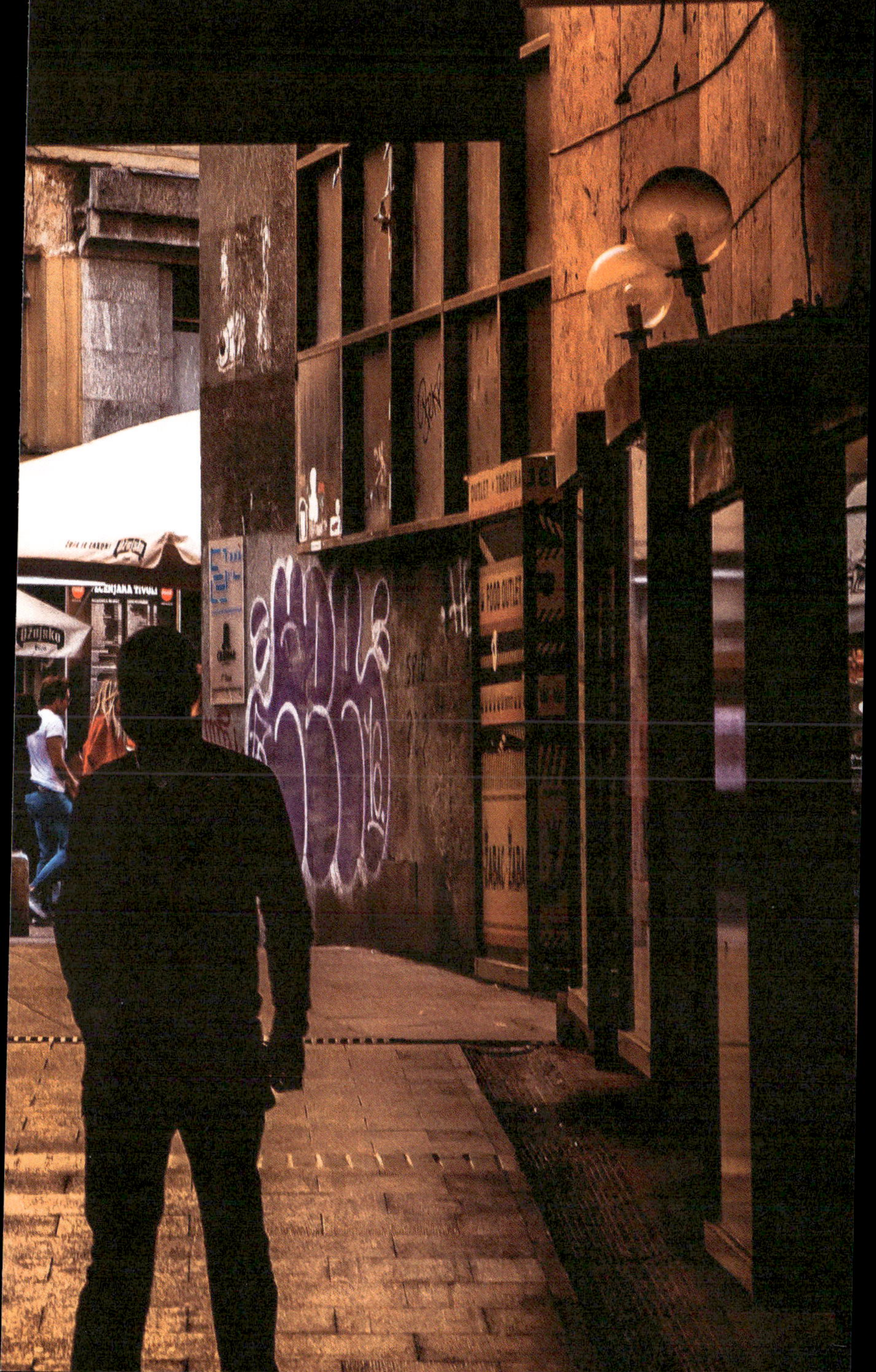

CPSIA information can be obtained at www.ICGtesting.com
Printed in the USA
BVIW120755300819
557142BV00019B/75